Rethinking
Ecofeminist Politics

Rethinking Ecofeminist <u>Politics</u>

by
Janet Biehl

South End Press   **Boston**

Cover art by Mandy Mastrovita
Text design and production by Tanya Mckinnon and South End Press
Printing corresponds to the last digit: 10 9 8 7 6 5 4 3 2 1

Library of Congress Catalog Card Number: 90-26835
Library of Congress Cataloging-in-Publication Data
Biehl, Janet
        Rethinking Ecofeminist Politics
        1. Feminist theory. 2. Human ecology.
3. Biehl, Janet. I. Title. II. Ecofeminist politics
HQ1190.B54 1990   305.42'01--dc20
ISBN 0-89608-391-8 (pbk)

ISBN 0-89608-392-6 (cloth)

South End Press, 116 St. Botolph St., Boston MA 02115

Table of Contents

	Acknowledgments	vii
	Introduction	1
1.	Problems in Ecofeminism	9
2.	The Neolithic Mystique	29
3.	Divine Immanence and the "Aliveness" of Nature	57
4.	Mythopoesis and the Irrational	81
5.	Dialectics in the Ethics of Social Ecology	105
6.	Women in Democratic Politics	131
	Endnotes	159
	Index	175

Acknowledgments

I am deeply grateful to Murray Bookchin for sharing the ideas of social ecology with me, and for his personal encouragement and support of my work. He has been an endearing friend and a perceptive adviser during the course of writing this book. I am pleased to contribute this work to the ideas of social ecology as a whole.

I also give my thanks to my fellow members of the Burlington Greens, to the Northern Vermont Greens, and to social ecologists in the Left Green Network for creating and sustaining the political culture in which this book was written. Special thanks are due to Chuck Morse, who graciously and uncomplainingly shouldered most of my responsibilities for the Left Green Network clearinghouse while I was working on this book.

I would also like to express my appreciation to Elizabeth Lawrence and Gary Sisco for their encouragement and support of my work, and for discussions of many important issues pertaining to this book. Thanks to Dan Chodorkoff and Paula Emery of the Institute for Social Ecology, and to Phyllis and Julius Jacobson, who published two of my articles in their journal *New Politics,* portions of which have been worked into this book.

Thanks to my editors at South End Press, Ellen Herman and Tanya Mckinnon, for their careful attention to this manuscript. I am also grateful to Steve Chase of South End for soliciting radical ecology manuscripts.

For his consistent support and publication of my work in *Our Generation* and for his encouragement of this project, I owe many thanks to Dimitri Roussopoulos of Black Rose Books.

None of these individuals bear responsibility for any errors of judgment or fact in this book.

Introduction

My main purpose in writing this book has been to defend the best ideals of feminism from a disquieting tendency that has arisen from within its midst—ecofeminism. This effort is one that I have found very painful to perform. There once was a time when it seemed to me—as it did to other women—that feminism and ecology stood to mutually enrich each other. It had been my earnest hope that ecofeminism would draw upon the best of social theory and meld it with radical concepts in ecology to produce a genuinely anti-hierarchical, enlightened, and broadly oppositional movement, one that could oppose sexism and the many forces that are at work in destroying the biosphere and trammeling human freedom. Its emphasis on women's sexual liberation as part of the "revolt of nature" seemed an exhilarating contribution to feminist theory. It seemed to promise a new integration of humanity's place in nonhuman nature, an appreciation of women's historical role in childbearing and childrearing, while at the same time emancipating women from regressive definitions that placed them exclusively in that social role. It seemed to provide feminists with a creative and thoughtful approach for building an ecological movement.

But recent ecofeminist literature does not fulfill this promise at all. It has not drawn on the best of previous social theory, but instead works in a realm outside it, even rejecting it as "male" or "masculine." It has not drawn on the best legacies of Western culture—and despite its many abuses, Western culture does have emancipatory legacies—but instead situates women outside Western culture altogether, associated with a mystified notion of "nature." It largely ignores or rejects legacies of democracy, of reason,

1

and of the project of scientifically understanding much of the natural world as part of a radical liberatory movement. For if women and nature are radically counterposed to Western culture, as many ecofeminists claim, this lodges women basically outside the best of that cultural legacy. It has thus become an ideology that, far from being liberatory, is regressive for most thinking women.

Ecofeminism has also become a force for irrationalism, most obviously in its embrace of goddess worship, its glorification of the early Neolithic, and its emphasis on metaphors and myths. It has also become irrational in another sense: that is, by virtue of its own incoherence. Although some book-length works have been written on themes pertaining to women and nature and have inspired ecofeminists—Mary Daly's *Gyn/Ecology,* Susan Griffin's *Woman and Nature,* Carolyn Merchant's *Death of Nature,* Andrée Collard's *Rape of the Wild*—to my knowledge, no sustained book-length account of ecofeminist theory itself has yet appeared. Instead, ecofeminist theory defines itself largely by a plethora of short, often self-contradictory essays on the subject. Such essays have been anthologized under the broad rubric of ecofeminism, most recently in Irene Diamond and Gloria Orenstein's *Reweaving the World: The Emergence of Ecofeminism* and in Judith Plant's *Healing the Wounds: The Promise of Ecofeminism.* A few basic themes run through most of the essays in these anthologies: an acceptance that "women and nature" are to be counterposed, almost without qualification, to Western culture; that women have an exclusive role in developing a sensibility of "caring" and "nurturing"; and that they are unique in their ability to appreciate humanity's "interconnectedness" with the natural world.

But apart from these basic themes, the short essays anthologized in these books often blatantly contradict each other. Some of the recent essays argue, for example, that there is an innate, even biological "connection" between women and nature, while others avow that this "connection" is really a socially constructed product. Some advocate a belief in a goddess, while others are adamantly secular. Some locate the roots of the ecological crisis in the late Neolithic in Europe, while others locate those roots in Christianity, and still others in the Scientific Revolution. Some assert that

"All is One," while others argue for particularism and multiplicity. Some are influenced by social ecology, while others have ties with deep ecology. Some regard ecofeminism as a liberatory concept of nearly unprecedented proportions, while others—even in articles in these anthologies themselves—reject the name "ecofeminism" altogether as insulting to feminist activists.

Although most political movements might feel the need to sort out these differences and their theorists might argue for and against them, producing a healthy debate, ecofeminists rarely confront each other on the differences in these writings. Ecofeminists who even acknowledge the existence of serious contradictions tend, in fact, to pride themselves on the contradictions in their works as a healthy sign of "diversity"—presumably in contrast to "dogmatic," fairly consistent, and presumably "male" or "masculine" theories. But dogmatism is clearly not the same thing as coherence, clarity, and at least a minimum level of consistency. Ecofeminism, far from being healthily diverse, is so blatantly self-contradictory as to be incoherent. As one might expect, at least one ecofeminist even rejects the very notion of coherence itself, arguing that coherence is "totalizing" and by inference oppressive. Moreover, because ecofeminists rarely debate each other, it is nearly impossible to glean from their writings the extent to which they agree or disagree with each other. The reader of this book should be wary of attributing the views of any one ecofeminist, as they are presented here, to all other ecofeminists. But ecofeminists' apparent aversion to sorting out the differences among themselves leaves the critical observer no choice but to generalize.

The self-contradictory nature of ecofeminism raises further problems as well. Some ecofeminists literally celebrate the identification of women with nature as an ontological reality. They thereby speciously biologize the personality traits that patricentric society assigns to women. The implication of this position is to confine women to the same regressive social definitions from which feminists have fought long and hard to emancipate women. Other ecofeminists reject such biologizations and rightly consider what are virtually sociobiological definitions of women as regressive for women.

But some of the same ecofeminists who reject these definitions *nonetheless favor using them to build a movement.* Even as
they reject them theoretically, even as they fail to confront
ecofeminists who accept them, they still disseminate the same
"woman-nature" metaphors. Indeed, the very existence of the
ecofeminist movement depends on some people believing in such
metaphors, whether their theorists regard them as ontologically
true or not. In my view, the notion of building a movement on
something one *knows* is a reactionary falsehood raises serious
moral questions about deception and manipulation, questions that
women in the ecology movement would do well to ask of
ecofeminists and that should be a matter of grave concern to serious
feminists today generally.

Some of the more highly visible ecofeminists have been well
served by this body of "ideas," leading to careers in academia and
on the ecology movement's lecture circuit. And from the sweeping
claims that ecofeminists make about "women and nature," one
might suppose that *every* woman who ever worked as an ecological
activist is at least a proto-ecofeminist, if not an outright ecofeminist—from Rachel Carson, to the Love Canal anti-toxics activists, to
the women of the Chipko "tree-hugging" movement in India, to
women in the bioregionalist, deep ecology, social ecology, Earth
First!, and other wings of the ecology movement. To be sure, some
activist women in these movements no doubt do identify themselves as ecofeminists.

As a feminist who finds the contradictions in ecofeminism
embarrassing, I resent the claim of ecofeminist writers to embrace
nearly every female ecological activist under their own rubric. It is
hardly likely that they *all* do. What is also of deep concern to me
is that many female ecological activists feel obliged to mute their
criticism due to subtle ecofeminist demands for gender solidarity—
in the name of an "ecofeminist imperative," as several ecofeminists
have put it—that verges on moral and intellectual coercion. In fact
it is not at all clear that for a woman to be a feminist and a radical
ecologist of any kind, she must also be an ecofeminist. Despite the
grandiose generalities about women and nature made by ecofeminist writers, it is eminently possible for a feminist who is also an

ecological activist not to adopt this often-problematic agglomeration of contradictory ideas.

I myself once wrote an article called "What Is Social Ecofeminism?" as an attempt to provide an alternative to "mainstream" ecofeminism.[1] In that article I drew primarily on the ideas of social ecology as they pertain to women, and I sought to show how women's concerns could be integrated into social ecology. I sought to construct a coherent, rational, democratic, and libertarian alternative under the rubric of "social ecofeminism." Other theorists, like Chiah Heller, have also worked toward developing a social ecofeminism. If there are still other women who wish to continue to work on that project, I certainly encourage them to do so.

But for my part, the very word *ecofeminism* has by now become so tainted by its various irrationalisms that I no longer consider this a promising project. I have no doubt that one can be a feminist who is deeply preoccupied with ecological questions, as I would hope there are many ecologically oriented people who regard the liberation of women as an integral part of their social agenda. But in my view, it hardly makes sense to build a movement on metaphors that I oppose and on confused ideas that I cannot formulate in any coherent manner. Nor do I consider it promising to work in a particularistic vein, advancing women as in any way the special custodians of nonhuman nature. Instead, since I am committed to the concept that ecology is a movement that should speak for a *general* interest of human beings *as a whole,* I primarily identify myself with social ecology—an antihierarchal, coherent, rational, and democratic body of ideas. Social ecology's dialectical approach to a clear understanding of hierarchy and domination—developed originally and still most fully by Murray Bookchin—is basic to my understanding of contemporary social and ecological problems.

As a form of eco-anarchism, social ecology's guiding precept is that we cannot rid ourselves today of the ideology of dominating nature until we rid ourselves of hierarchy and class structures in human society—including not only sexism and homophobia and racism, but also the nation-state, economic exploitation, capitalism, and all the other social oppressions of our time. Neither nonhuman nature nor humanity will cease to be subject to domination until every human being is free of domination. In this respect women are objects of domination but not the sole or primary objects of domination. It is only by eliminating domination as such—including the domination of man by man—both as idea and reality that women will be able to fulfill themselves completely, not only as gendered beings, but as *human* beings.

The early radical feminism of the late 1960s and early 1970s—which most inspires me—called for the equality of women in *every* aspect of social and domestic life. The more radical feminists who initiated that movement recognized that the full equality of women could not be achieved without far-reaching changes in all structures of society. By contrast, ecofeminism's sweeping but highly confused cosmology introduces magic, goddesses, witchcraft, privileged quasi-biological traits, irrationalities, Neolithic atavisms, and mysticism into a movement that once tried to gain the best benefits of the Enlightenment and the most valuable features of civilization for women, on a par with thinking and humane men. What were once seen by progressive thinkers as the general goals of humanity as a whole, to be attained without any gender restrictions, have been dissolved by ecofeminists into a body of vague parochial notions focused overwhelmingly on women's allegedly special quasi-biological traits and a mystical relationship that they presumably have with nature—a "nature" conceived as an all-nurturing and domestic Great Mother. This highly disparate body of hazy, poorly formulated notions, metaphors, and irrational analogies invites women *to take a step backward* to an era whose consciousness was permeated by myths and by mystifications of reality. It does not bode well for women—especially those who regard themselves as more than creatures of their sexuality—to follow in this regressive path.

Social ecology, with its eco-anarchist, anti-hierarchical approach, argues for the need to raise once again the social and intellectual questions that the early radical feminist movement raised—including women's need to go beyond the domestic realm into a new politics for radical social change. In its call for the abolition of hierarchy as such, social ecology reveals the countless forms of domination that afflict women in all areas and walks of life, whether they are in the family, the state, the church—including attempts to regard them, however "reverently," as earth mothers, priestesses, magicians, or more conventionally, as the guardians of Victorian morality. Embracing metaphors that associate women with nonhuman nature, far from being ecological, are actually mystifications of oppressive patriarchal stereotypes. That this process of mystification is widespread today is no accident, in view of the sweeping disempowerment of people, the erosion of human community ties in the Western and non-Western worlds, and ubiquitous flights into escapism and mythopoesis.

As a woman and a feminist, I deeply value my power of rationality and seek to expand the full range of women's faculties. I do not want to reject the valuable achievements of Western culture on the claim that they have been produced primarily by men. The music of Beethoven is as dear to me as the poetry of Emily Dickinson. We cannot dispense with millennia of that culture's complex social, philosophical, and political developments—including democracy and reason—because of the many abuses that are intertwined with that culture.

Whether one agrees with me that social ecology is the best alternative or not, it is my hope that this book will open up a serious debate about ecofeminism in the ecology and feminist movements, on questions that have gone unaddressed for far too long. At the very least, I hope it will carve out a space for women who are working in the ecology movement so that they can free themselves from "the ecofeminist imperative"—indeed, to resist its moralistic obscurantism—and to think for themselves.

Burlington, Vermont
October 7, 1990

Chapter 1

Problems in Ecofeminism

A major historical nemesis of women's liberation has been the theory of biological determinism, the notion that differences between the sexes are rooted in an eternal female biology. At least since Mary Wollstonecraft, it has been the feminist project to refute sexist ideologies and show that they are the product of social factors, not biology. When scientists have tried to provide biological bases for differences between the sexes—by measuring cranial size, or attributing determinative force to hormones—feminists have traditionally shown that these scientific "experiments" simply reinforce institutions and ideologies of women's subjugation and justify women's exclusion from civic life. When sociobiological justifications of androcentrism build reproductive differences into elaborate theories of "female nature," feminists have traditionally shown that they unjustly shore up sexist institutions and ideologies.

Ecofeminism, largely influenced by Mary Daly's kind of cultural feminism of the 1970s, has consciously departed from this traditional feminist approach. Liberation for women, ecofeminists generally argue, does not require that women "sever" themselves from their sexual and reproductive biology or from "nature." Although traditional feminists admirably "dismantled the iron grip of biological determinism," as ecofeminists Irene Diamond and Gloria Orenstein acknowledge, in fighting biological determinism they seemed to insist that "women would not be free until the

9

connections between women and the natural world were severed."[1]
Shulamith Firestone's *Dialectic of Sex*—which argued in the early
1970s that reproduction should become a technological affair,
removed from women's biology altogether—epitomized the "anti-
natural," antibiological tendency of feminism, in ecofeminist eyes.
But women need not anathematize their biology to be free,
ecofeminists argue. Ynestra King rejects Firestone's "removal of
biological reproduction from women's bodies as a condition for
women's liberation," as well as what she calls the "rationalist
radical feminism" that asserts that "the woman-nature identification is a male ideology and a tool of oppression which must itself
be overcome."[2] King, in fact, often writes that women need not
"sever" the "woman-nature connection" as a precondition for their
liberation.

Let me state what I generally agree with in the ecofeminist
literature. Most obviously, ecofeminists and all feminists argue that
women have been subordinated to one degree or another throughout the long history of Western culture and in most other cultures
as well. It is true, as ecofeminists argue, that women's reproductive
and sexual biology itself is not the source of women's oppression,
but rather the hierarchies that many men have built on them. There
is no doubt that women's biology has long been seen as inferior to
men's and that this alleged inferiority was long used as a justification for women's exclusion from full participation in social life.
Rather, as ecofeminists argue, women's biology is not only a fact—
is not only necessary—it can be itself a source of liberation, especially in sexuality. Sexual liberation—including the liberation of
women's bodies—is extremely important for the liberation of
women. Women's liberation undoubtedly depends on their sexual
freedom and the full realization of their sensuality. Many women
do find childbearing and childrearing a source of great and genuine
satisfaction. It is certainly true that women have historically played
an extremely important role in socializing infants and rearing
children, a role that has not been sufficiently appreciated.
Ecofeminists are thus quite right to stress that women should not
despise their own reproductive and sexual biology. To acknowledge obvious physical differences between people—whether in

gender or in ethnicity—need not lead inevitably to hierarchy. "Whether we want it or not, we have a social and biological matrix," ecofeminist Susan Griffin rightly argues.[3] One may indeed be a "historical agent" with reproductive organs that are different from those of men.

And it is true, as ecofeminists argue, that contemporary Western culture does not have a sense of its dependency on the biosphere, and that it is relentlessly befouling both its nest and the rest of the world. It is indeed not liberating for women or anyone else to become as domineering and exploitative as many men currently are. Ecofeminists properly warn us that to simply integrate women into the hierarchical structures of the existing society—corporations, government, political parties—is not a radical solution. Let there be no doubt that an ecological society would be one in which nurturing and caring would be highly prized. And the struggle to preserve community life in both Western and non-Western cultures is a valiant one that should be supported wholeheartedly. Where cultural feminism long wrestled with the problem of racism—its theory of the primary oppression of women did not seem to admit racism as an oppression of equal importance—ecofeminism has been able to appeal to women across racial and cultural lines on the basis of its critique of Western culture and the export of Western-style development to Third World countries.[4]

Psycho-Biologistic Ecofeminists

But serious problems begin to arise when some ecofeminists come to regard certain *personality* aspects of women as innate. Indeed, ecofeminism's healthy impulse to reclaim women's biology has in many cases become an acceptance of some of the same constricting stereotypes of "women's nature" that have long been used to oppress them. When ecofeminists root women's personality traits in reproductive and sexual biology, they tend to give acceptance to those male-created images that define women as primarily biological beings. For Andrée Collard, for example, to say that woman's reproductive biology is "the wellspring of her strength" is to deliver women over to the male stereotypes that root women's character structure entirely in their biological being:

> Nothing links the human animal and nature so *profoundly* as woman's *reproductive system* which enables her to share the experience of bringing forth and nourishing life with the rest of the living world. Whether or not she personally experiences biological mothering, it is in this that woman is most truly a child of nature and in this natural integrity lies *the wellspring of her strength.* (emphasis added)[5]

In fact, psycho-biological ecofeminists believe that women, owing to their biological makeup, have an innately more "caring" and "nurturing" way of being than men, a view that roots their parenting attributes in a uniquely genetic makeup. Unlike other feminists, who tried to demolish gender stereotypes as insufferably constraining to women's development as full human beings, such ecofeminists enthusiastically begin to embrace some of these same psycho-biological stereotypes.

That "nurturing" characteristics that the present society presumably despises are in fact badly needed now if we are to overcome our ecological crisis is indisputable. But are these characteristics as biologically innate in women as psycho-biological ecofeminists claim? And are serious feminists to accept images of women as "emotional," "caring," and "mediating," in contradistinction to men in a presumably shared ecology movement or in building a new society? Is women's personality integrally tied to their biology, as psycho-biological ecofeminists claim? And is the enemy of women the all-embracing "white male" Western civilization that devalues them?

This psycho-biologistic approach to what is often a complex, culturally-conditioned interpretation of women's behavioral traits often leads to a strange mixture of male-created values with psycho-biologistic identifications of women with nonhuman nature. Nearly all ecofeminists, whether they are psycho-biological or not, draw on the idea that women have long been "associated with nature," in Western culture, by males. It is not merely that women have done the work of transforming "nature" into "culture," of rearing children, caring for the household, and the like. Rather, most ecofeminists believe, women have been "associated with nature" in a way that is deep-seated, a way that not only perpetuates the subordination of women but is at the root of the ecological crisis. The earth, they point out, was long called "Mother Earth" in ancient Mediterranean cultures because of "her" agricultural fertility and seasonal cyclicity. The Homeric Hymn to "Earth, the Mother of All," to take another example, is a paean of praise to the responsiveness of the earth to tillage. Hesiod's cosmogony, or account of the origin of the universe and culture, describes a progression from the generative powers of the female Gaia ("wide-bosomed earth") to the moral authority of the male god Zeus. Western literary imagery that deals with males and females has often been polarized in gender terms. Indeed, so much do most ecofeminists assume that women and nonhuman nature have been "associated" that they refer to the "woman-nature connection" or even "woman equals nature" as if no further examination of this question were needed.

That such associations were created by patriarchal and patricentric cultures to debase women does not deter psycho-biologistic ecofeminists from consciously identifying themselves with nonhuman nature itself. They are often inspired by Griffin, an early ecofeminist writer, who proclaimed, "We know ourselves to be made from this earth. We know this earth is made from our bodies. For we see ourselves. And we *are* nature. We are *nature seeing nature.* We are nature with a concept of nature. Nature weeping. Nature speaking of nature to nature." (emphasis added)[6] For psycho-biologistic ecofeminists, women are uniquely attuned to the "interconnectedness" and "cycles" of nonhuman nature. Charlene Spretnak, for example, writes that biological aspects of women's sexuality make it possible for "mysteries" of nature to be "revealed" to them: "The intensities of that mystery [of the cosmic unfolding] are revealed to us during the postorgasmic state," by which she means a sensation of "boundarylessness" that only women supposedly experience after orgasm (an assertion that would come as a surprise to many men). "The experiences inherent in women's sexuality," she continues, "are expressions of the essential, holistic nature of life on Earth; they are 'body parables' of the profound oneness and interconnectedness of all matter/energy, which physicists have discovered in recent decades at the subatomic level."[7]

It must be confessed that psycho-biologistic ecofeminism reaches perhaps its most baroque proportions in the writings of Spretnak, who seeks not merely a friendly attitude toward women's reproductive biology but a comprehensive biological definition of women as ecological beings. She advises women to follow other "body parables" of their sexuality that can be found in the "moon-rhythm blood of menses," not to speak of "reclaimed menstruation, orgasm, pregnancy, natural childbirth, and motherhood." Spretnak, who regards the earth as a female deity, conceptualizes "the goddess" in terms of a veritable geography of women's biology. Spretnak's goddess has her "womblike caves," her "voluptuous contours and fertile plains," and "her flowing waters that give life, [and] her animal teachers." The goddess teaches "lessons of cyclic renewal and regeneration."[8]

To be sure, not all ecofeminists follow Spretnak in biologizing women as presumably uniquely ecological beings. But it has been a keystone of most ecofeminist writings that women and "nature" have been "associated" by virtue of being "other" to Western culture. This idea can be traced back to Simone de Beauvoir, who wrote in *The Second Sex:*

> Man *seeks* in woman the Other as Nature and as his fellow being. But we know what ambivalent feelings Nature inspires in man. He exploits her, but she crushes him, he is born of her and dies in her; she is the source of his being and the realm that he subjugates to his will; Nature is a vein of gross material in which the soul is imprisoned, and she is the supreme reality; she is contingence and Idea, the finite and the whole; she is what opposes the Spirit, and the Spirit itself. Now ally, now enemy, she appears as the dark chaos from whence life wells up, as this life itself, and as the

over-yonder toward which life tends. Woman
sums up Nature as Mother, Wife, and Idea; these
forms now mingle and now conflict, and each of
them wears a *double visage* . (emphasis added)[9]

Nearly all ecofeminists—psycho-biologistic or otherwise—
agree with the idea that women and nature have not only been
"associated" but have been seen as "other" by Western culture.
They do not see that these associations and ambivalences are
precisely what "man seeks in woman" and in nature, as de Beauvoir
saw; rather, they extol women as "other" with nonhuman nature in
a crude exaggeration of her subtle exposition. The rich and complex
dialectical insights of de Beauvoir's passage, in which women and
nature have a "double visage," are reduced to a single visage—as
forces outside culture, to be feared and dominated. Indeed,
ecofeminists make these "male" characterizations into a veritable
ideology that roots women outside Western culture altogether. This
may take extremely crude forms, as when Ynestra King writes
algebraically of a "woman equals nature connection." The male-
created joint "otherness" of women, in which "woman equals
nature," in fact becomes a *positive* political starting point for
ecofeminists. For King, women as ecofeminists are "the revolutionary bearers...of antidualistic potential in the world today" by *virtue
of* their joint "otherness." To Judith Plant, so intimate is this
common "otherness" that it even suggests a nondualistic epistemology, for "feeling the life of the 'other'—literally experiencing
its existence—is becoming the new starting point for human decision-making."[10]

Despite ecofeminism's allegedly "revolutionary" potential,
some feminists (who are *not* ecofeminists) have criticized
ecofeminism and its closely associated cultural feminism for their
reactionary implications. Ecofeminist images of women, these crit-
ics correctly warn, retain the patriarchal stereotypes of what men
expect women to be. These stereotypes freeze women as merely
caring and nurturing beings, instead of expanding the full range of
women's human potentialities and abilities. To focus overwhelmingly on women's "caring nature" as the source of ecologically

necessary "values" easily leads to the notion that women are to remain intuitive and discourages them from expanding their human horizons and capacities.[11]

It is important to note that de Beauvoir flatly repudiated "the new femininity" such as ecofeminism offers, criticizing its return to an

> enhanced status for traditional feminine values, such as women and her rapport with nature, woman and her maternal instinct, woman and her physical being...This renewed attempt to pin women down to their *traditional role,* together with a small effort to meet some of the demands made by women—that's the formula used to try and keep women quiet. *Even women who call themselves feminists don't always see through it.* Once again, women are being defined in terms of "the other," once again they are being made into the "second sex."...Equating ecology with feminism is something that irritates me. They are not automatically one and the same thing at all. (emphasis added)[12]

De Beauvoir's well-placed emphasis on the "traditional role" assigned to women by male-created cultures is a conclusion that can only be highly disconcerting to ecofeminism, for it was from this pioneer in women's liberation that ecofeminists borrowed their basic concept of the "otherness" of women and nature. That it is now women—and not men—who define women as "other" with nature is a milestone in the passage in recent decades from a struggle for women's liberation to assertions of mere female chauvinism in ecofeminism.

The fact is that Western associations of women with nonhuman nature—or as closer to nonhuman nature than men—were enormously debasing to women. Ancient Greek culture excluded women from political life because of their presumed intellectual inferiority; Aristotle wrote that their *logos* or reason "lacks authority." Plato believed that in the origin of the two sexes, women result when men who do not do well in their life on earth come back through transmigration of the soul as females.[13] Euripides in a fragment says that "woman is a more terrible thing than the violence of the raging sea, than the force of torrents, than the sweeping breath of fire."[14] Semonides delivered a diatribe comparing what he saw as various types of women to various animals. Ancient Roman law regarded women as having a "levity of mind," and in Christian culture, Augustine saw women as "weaker." Eve came to be seen as a temptress for her role in the Fall—in the words of the Christian father Tertullian, "the gateway to hell." Aquinas, following Aristotle, regarded women as "misbegotten" and defective. The association of women with nonhuman nature or as beings closer to nonhuman nature has thus been immensely degrading for women, contributing to untold misery in the lives of countless women in Western culture.

Social Constructionist Ecofeminists

Some ecofeminists, in the light of this problem, have disclaimed the notion that women's "caring" and "nurturing" are biologically based attributes. They assert that the woman-nature association is a *social construction,* an ideology that is the product of men. For Susan Griffin, men in our "split culture" construct women and nature as "other" because they "fear" the fact that they "are Nature." Similarly, for Ynestra King, the "woman = nature connection" is a result of men's fear of "the fact that they are born of women and are dependent upon non-human nature."[15] For King, "woman = nature" is "socially constructed," and "the idea that women are closer to nature is an ideology. It's not true. It was made up by men as a way to sentimentalize and devalue both....It's a masculine definition." This represents a puzzling contradiction to King's other writings, where, as we have seen, she has *criticized* what she calls "rationalist radical feminism" for asserting that "the woman-nature identification is a male ideology and a tool of oppression which must itself be overcome."[16]

Other social-constructionist ecofeminists, by contrast, have consistently asserted that the "woman-nature association" is based on purely cultural images, not on women's biological reality. So-cialist ecofeminist Carolyn Merchant, for example, has long argued that "any analysis that makes women's essence and qualities spe-cial ties them to a biological destiny that thwarts the possibility of liberation. A politics grounded in women's culture, experience, and values can be seen as reactionary." Indeed, Merchant's socialist ecofeminism views "both nature and human nature as historically and socially constructed."[17]

Still other ecofeminists seem unable to decide on the issue of psycho-biology versus social construction one way or the other. Judith Plant, for example, writes that "women have been socialized in such a way that allows them to experience compassion" and that "the subjugation of women and nature is a social construction, not a biologically determined fact." Yet this does not prevent her from speaking elsewhere, in a psycho-biological vein, of "women's val-ues" as "centered around life-giving."[18] Eerie contradictions may even appear within the same work by a single ecofeminist author. Andrée Collard, for example, is unclear about whether nature itself even exists at all, or if it is a cultural convention. In one passage in her book *Rape of the Wild* she argues that "participation in nature is based upon a recognition of the reality that nature exists of, for, and by herself." Indeed, she criticizes male hunters for seeing nonhuman nature in terms of images, instead of as it really is. But in another passage, she asserts that "nature is a state of mind and a cultural convention." Indeed, "reality is in the mind's eye."[19]

Social-constructionist ecofeminists are rather unusual in their invocation of regressive metaphors to build an ostensibly liberatory movement. Blacks, for example, do not organize themselves against racism by using the metaphors of "laziness" and "shiftlessness" that were long used to buttress racism, but somehow these ecofeminists seem to think that comparably regressive metaphors can be liberating for women. Metaphors have, in fact, become a favored province for social-constructionist ecofeminists when it comes not only to the subject of women but also to the subject of nature. Metaphors of women as "nurturing"—presumably like the earth—and of the earth as female abound. For Plant, "the rape of the earth, in all its forms, becomes a *metaphor* for the rape of woman, in all its many guises."[20] Merchant speaks of "the *metaphor* of the earth as a nurturing mother [that] was gradually to vanish as a dominant image."[21]

Ironically, the shift to social constructionism has somewhat diminished the original ecofeminist passion to reclaim "nature" in an organic sense—certainly when it comes to women's biology. Yet in dissolving "women and nature" into metaphors or subjective attributes, social-constructionist ecofeminists obscure both nonhuman nature and women's relationship to it. They leave undefined the way women, as human beings, gradually evolved out of non-human nature, while remaining part of nature as a whole. One wonders how many ecofeminists can claim to "speak for" a "nature" that they perceive as illusory or only through metaphors.

Viewed as a whole, then, ecofeminism raises perplexing problems for its adherents. On the one hand, there are ecofeminists who make psycho-biological claims about women's presumably more ecological nature and values. On the other hand, there are ecofeminists who insist that these very traits are either illusory, useful fictions, or socially contructed—not biologically intrinsic. Still others seem to maintain *both* views at once, apparently without recognizing that they are contradictory. Unless coherence and logic are to be thoroughly despised, readers of ecofeminist writings may well ask what these differing tendencies in ecofeminism have in common. Is it a reverence for women's inherent biological traits, or an attempt to show that these traits are merely social constructions and eliminate them? Or dare I suggest that ecofeminism is simply incoherent, contradictory, and sharply at odds with itself?

In any case, try as it may, ecofeminism cannot have its cake and eat it too. In a time of sweeping mystification, when reality is transformed into myth and myth transformed into reality—indeed, when even the very reality of the world itself is challenged as merely subjective, as Collard does—one may reasonably wonder whether ecofeminism is clarifying the relationship of women to nature or muddling it.

Ecofeminism and Ethics

For millennia, Western culture was embedded in an organic ethical nexus in which the market occupied a secondary and indeed marginal place. Small-scale village life long consisted of communities that perceived themselves as existing not for the sake of individual gratification but for a higher purpose—whether it was to serve a deity or to serve the community itself. However much this perception may have been honored in the breach, for such cultures, nature in the sense of the cosmos had a prescriptive ethical force that not only organized society along "naturalistic" lines but that also prevented the market economy from invading the society as a whole. Whether we speak of organic societies, tribes, villages, or even city-states and feudal communes, they were highly integrated and marked by strong bonds of mutual aid at the base of society, even when hierarchical political or religious structures loomed over them.

But the emergence of capitalism fragmented these communities, and the moral or religious ties that integrated them were subverted by a market economy based on self-interest and an instrumental mentality that was placed in its service. This constellation of factors denuded society of its naturalistic ethical content. The ethic of the merely instrumental and utilitarian now began to assume ascendancy over values that had been more organic and naturalistic in character. Such a utilitarian framework judged and continues to judge everything—human and nonhuman alike—by the criterion of its usefulness. The value of people and nonhuman nature lies in their utility in attaining a given end, such as economic supremacy or political power. Within the present culture, social theorist Gina Blumenfeld has written, "there is no greater expression of the domination of human over human than the reduction of human beings to objects of utility—to means of production or instruments of pleasure."[22] The operationalist norm of "whatever works, is right" has replaced any sense of higher meaning in human life. In the twentieth century, the "good" has devolved into a matter of personal preference and choice. The era when an objective ethics grounded in nature was possible seems irretrievably lost.

Yet surely human life means more than simply to be a cog in a machine. Surely the wealth of human subjectivities demands a culture that has ethical meaning. Surely there should be more to life than a system in which humans are used for their instrumental value—as workers, as slaves, as "natural resources," as objects of exploitation and domination. Surely women are more than household servants and childrearers. Surely men are more than cannon fodder for wars, atoms whose needs are served by immense bureaucracies. Surely people are more than instruments.

The same instrumentalism—driven by the capitalist law of "grow or die," accumulate or be devoured by a rival—reduced nonhuman nature to a mere resource for exploitation as well. The ecology question thus raises once again the need for an objective ethics. As most radical ecologists understand, the ecological crisis cannot be solved simply by motivations of self-interest, much less by the moral nihilism propagated by fashionable postmodernist theorists. By themselves, social forces—or "laws," as economists put it—will not solve the ecological crisis in a liberatory way. Nor can it be solved by a utilitarian or operationalist ethical framework—by "what works"—for "what works" has been one of the ideologies that has clearly contributed to ecological destruction and that has also justified the "efficiency" of highly totalitarian political systems. Nor can "ecocapitalism" (a form of merchandising with a green patina) arrest the ravages of the ever-expanding market economy, for it is precisely that economic system, as social ecologist Murray Bookchin has argued, that lies at the root of the ecological crisis today. It will take an effort of coherent human purpose, of intensely conscious moral agency, to end the destruction of the biosphere, based on an understanding of humanity's place in nature.

We must once again find an ethics somehow grounded in objectivity—which in our culture is the cosmos, nature—on the basis of which we can establish an ethical ecological society. Various sorts of ecologists are attempting to reintroduce ethics into radical discourse: it is in fact an important project for all ecological philosophy of this day. For example, deep ecology theorists assert that every life-form has "intrinsic value." For them, this view means that every organism has the "right" to fulfill itself and realize all its needs in the natural world. Social ecology theorists, in turn, see nature as a graded phenomenon in which biological nature (or "first nature") forms the basis for an emerging, uniquely human social or "second nature." The unity of first and second nature into what Bookchin calls a "free" or "self-conscious" nature, expressed by human agency, produces an ethics of complementarity in which various life-forms, including humans, complement each other in new ecological communities rather than conflict with each other.

Like these other kinds of ecologists, ecofeminists too are trying to develop an ecological ethics. The primary values that ecofeminists are interested in instilling in society are, of course, caring and nurturing, whether biologically based or socially con-structed in women. Writes Judith Plant, "Women's values, centered around life-giving, must be revalued, elevated from their once subordinate role. What women know from experience needs recog-nition and respect."[23] Ecofeminists also seek to instill a value for life. The destruction of the biosphere, as they see it, is in great measure brought about by a disrespect, fear, and even hatred of all that is living. Instead of the "necrophilic" dominant culture, ecofeminism seeks to infuse society with this value for life. More-over, they seek a world that is peaceful: militarism and the patriar-chal warrior, for ecofeminists, have played a large role in devaluing and destroying life, women, and the biosphere. Women, by con-trast, are more peaceful, whether for biological or social reasons.

Interconnectedness is still another—and perhaps the most primary—of the ecological values that ecofeminists commonly prescribe. They seek to recover a sense of the interconnectedness of life, to instil a sense of the human as part of the web of life, as part of a whole. Diamond and Orenstein call for "an experiential ethic of ecological interconnectedness." Starhawk also offers inter-connectedness a value for ecofeminism. Such arguments have been recycled in a multitude of articles by ecofeminists.[24]

In seeking an ethical ground on which to base these values, ecofeminists take a variety of approaches. For some ecofeminists, the ethical ground is simply the caring ethos of women themselves, in the *oikos* or domestic realm. Judith Plant, who believes that women's "caring" nature is socially constructed, nonetheless argues that "women's values are centered around life-giving" and seeks to revalue the "source of [society's] humanness," the domestic realm.[25]

Other ecofeminists seek nothing less than a new cosmology as a ground for their ecological ethics. While correctly observing that previous societies did not devastate the biosphere the way present-day societies are doing, they point to the ethical restraints that these societies had placed on economic and technological developments. Some ecofeminists call for a revival of the view of "nature" (presumably inorganic as well as organic) as literally alive in their attempt to restore an ethical cosmology. For Starhawk, a belief in the "aliveness" of the earth will instill a sense of caring and interconnectedness:

> When we understand that the Earth itself embodies spirit and that the cosmos is alive, then we also understand that everything is interconnected. Just as in our bodies: what happens to a finger affects what happens to a toe.[26]

To see nature as a living organism, for such ecofeminists, seems to restore a sacred character to nonhuman nature. Moreover, the cyclicity of the earth is to teach a contrary lesson to Western culture's belief in "linear progress," which ecofeminists often see as a large factor in the destruction of the biosphere, an approach that virtually equates any progress in history with an anti-ecological mentality. Not surprisingly, this ensemble of beliefs leads ecofeminists to uncritically and ahistorically romanticize *prehistoric* cultures that believed in the "aliveness" of the earth or of "nature" as a whole. Among the prehistoric cultures ecofeminists find to be memorable are the early Neolithic in Eastern Europe and Minoan Crete. To remember these lost cultures, we are often told, is to cultivate the values ecofeminists prize:

> The postpatriarchal options that we are evolving
> have roots in the peaceful, egalitarian,
> body-honoring, Earth-revering, gynocentric
> cultures. To remember our potentials and to begin
> to live these possibilities with our sisters and
> brothers as we initiate change is our *political*
> process...Peaceful and progressive societies
> thrived for millennia where gynocentric values
> prevailed... In short, we have lived sanely before,
> we can do it again.(emphasis added)[27]

To equate "our political process" with recollections and a
revival of Neolithic, presumably "gynocentric" values, raises problems that I must defer to a later discussion. Suffice it to say here
that many ecofeminists believe that we can "remember" the values
of the Neolithic by adopting what they believe to have been the
religion of the Neolithic. Not all ecofeminists, to be sure, advocate
belief in a deity. But for the very many who do, the "immanence"
of the goddess that presumably was worshipped in Paleolithic and
early Neolithic Europe is the goddess' all-important characteristic.
For these ecofeminists, it is belief in an immanent deity that can
instill a sense of the "aliveness" of the earth and of the interconnectedness of all living beings.

Despite some ecofeminist claims that they are dedicated to
overcoming "otherness," many of these values that other
ecofeminists propose bear a striking resemblance to the traits that
patricentric society has always assigned to women. When it comes
to the question of constructing an ecological ethics, the problem of
clashing views in ecofeminism becomes a crucial issue. "Nature"
has long had force as an ecological ethic precisely because it has
also been regarded as *objective. Insofar as the ecofeminist bases for
ethics—interconnectedness, aliveness, "women's caring"—are mediated by the metaphors of "woman = nature," they avoid the
problem of objectivity in the real world.* Thus, if an ethic is to be
based strictly on metaphors, it becomes wholly tenuous. Metaphors
are at best marked by their vagueness, by their lack of an assured
connection with reality. Even in poetry, they are meant to leave

things ineffable, often to "reason" by analogy with undefinable experiences. In such cases the undefinable replaces the definable, the intuitive replaces the rational, and a vague image of reality replaces reality itself. It is clear that no ethics can be built on arbitrary and indefinable symbols. Either an ethics must be explicated in clear terms, if it is to be a meaningful guide to behavior, or else it remains dangerously fuzzy, or it provides no guide at all, leaving behavior purely to arbitrary matters of personal judgment and taste, however poetic—or reactionary—the metaphors may be.

The Eternal Feminine

The attempt by ecofeminists to formulate a new ontological ground for an ecological ethics on metaphors may be a failure from a rational viewpoint, but it may be a flaming success in another, ugly way—namely, by reinforcing gender stereotypes. If metaphors of nature cannot form the basis of an ecological ethics, metaphors of women as "nature," alas, are all too likely to provide the basis for sexist notions of women. Sexist characterizations like "intuitive," "irrational," "hysterical," and "unpredictable" have been slapped on women for centuries. At the very least, this should warn women about the reckless use of metaphors in trying to formulate an ecofeminist ethics.

If we are going to base an ethics on biologically fixed attributes of female behavior, then we are assuming that those attributes are necessarily eternal. For ecofeminists, women's caring and nurturing functions have presumably been so long-lived and so extensive, and their "association with nature" so longstanding that their own "nature" is ostensibly sufficiently permanent to be constituted as a ground for an ethics. Unlike the empires that are built up, then crumble to dust, women's "caring nature"—like the biosphere of the earth—supposedly stays the same. It may be damaged by the incursions of men and male society, to be sure, but it remains constant, loving, and immemorial. Ecofeminists, in fact, depend on the eternality of women's "nature" to guarantee that women will be the same peace-loving, ecological creatures now that they sup-

posedly were in the remote Neolithic. Despite the social constructionism of some ecofeminists, it is women's "caringness" that gives
women ("associated with nature") of 1990s Western culture a link
with women ("associated with nature") in the Neolithic. Somehow
everything is in "flux," as process philosophers have said—except
women. Women's "eternal" nature, whether biological or socially
constructed, gives them a unique status among ecofeminists not
only in the biosphere but in the entire cosmos.

For instrumental reasons—such as saving the biosphere—the
overall message of ecofeminism is that women are expected to
accept this constricted and eternalized definition of their humanity. Whether they want this unenviable, even stagnant cosmic
status is dubious, to say the least. Once again, women are being
asked to take the fall—this time, to save the planet. They have to
limit themselves to a constricted concept of an immutable or eternal
"female nature" that allows for no development and carves their
personalities in stone. Must women's potentialities for growth and
development be sacrificed to save the biosphere? In an age that is
at least somewhat more enlightened than the Neolithic, one would
think otherwise. One would suppose that it would be possible for
women to try to work as ecological radicals without having to
sacrifice the fulfillment of their personhood as part of an ever-de-
veloping universal humanity.

If women are to gain an understanding of their relationship
with nonhuman nature that is liberatory, it certainly cannot be done
by advancing a myth of the eternal feminine. Important as caring
and nurturing undoubtedly are, humanity, it is to be hoped, has
greater potentialities than caring and nurturing alone. What of such
goals as *consciousness, reason, and above all freedom?*

It actually changes very little to propound certain metaphors
about women—and then attempt to elude their consequences by
claiming that they are social constructions. Ecofeminism's attach-
ment to its own metaphors leaves the movement itself without any
clear understanding of women's and men's actual relationship to
nonhuman nature, let alone of women's and men's actual relationship to each other. Even as some ecofeminists reject the categories
of "otherness," their understanding of history greatly depends on

them. By accepting, even celebrating, a male-derived image of "woman = nature" ecofeminists do not define women's place in the cultural wealth of the West but exclude them from it. Ecofeminism, in effect, "nurtures" a new form of "otherness"—the image of women as simplistically and genetically other to Western culture. Hence, ecofeminism leaves women with none of the important liberatory legacies of Western culture—its democratic tradition, its quest to understand how nonhuman and human nature interact, its high regard for the individual, its fight against superstition, its high ideals of rationality, and the like. Even ecofeminists who reject male-derived categories of female "otherness" leave us with a historical legacy based *only* on women's "otherness" in an atavistic sense—and that, as we shall see, is a very slender thread indeed, and one fraught with many problems.

Chapter 2

The Neolithic Mystique

As early as the days of Hesiod, people discontented with Western society have yearned for a "golden age" which possesses simpler lifeways that are appealing. Many ecofeminists, too, propose an historical "golden age": a female-oriented society that was peaceful, gender-equal, and nature-loving in the early Neolithic period in Europe. Between 7000 B.C.E. and 3500 B.C.E., their interpretation runs, people in "Old Europe" lived in sedentary societies that revered nature. War was alien; their settlements were peaceful and harmonious. Society was gender-equal, and people worshipped an immanent "nature goddess" or a "Great Goddess" rather than "transcendent" sky gods. Although the society was matricentric, neither sex dominated the other—values were "gylanic," in Riane Eisler's terminology. These societies "were *not* warlike, they were *not* societies where women were subordinate. And they did *not* see our Earth as an object for exploitation and domination." In an ecstatic moment, Eisler writes that in that time "the world was one," and "the beating of drums was the heartbeat of the Earth—in all its mystery, enchantment, wonder, and terror. Our feet danced in sacred groves, honoring the spirits of nature....There was no splintering of culture and nature, spirituality, science, and technology" as there is today.[1]

Unlike the 19th-century scholar Jacob Bachofen, who relied almost entirely on classical mythology and female figurines to propose a theory of "matriarchy" in prehistory, these ecofeminists draw on the work of archaeologists to substantiate their claims. For the early Neolithic generally, the ecofeminists rely heavily on the work of archaeologist Marija Gimbutas, who studied a cluster of Neolithic cultures in southeastern Europe that do appear to have been relatively egalitarian, peaceful, and sex-equal.[2] In particular, Gimbutas studied the Vinca culture, an agricultural village that thrived in the sixth and fifth millennia B.C.E. in what is now Yugoslavia. Gimbutas labeled this cluster of cultures "Old Europe." She leaped to the arguable conclusion that the various fish, bird, and other symbols she found in the culture's artwork were symbols of a regenerative, life-giving goddess who had been worshipped there. Like every Eden, the ecofeminist Eden also fell. Beginning around 4500 B.C.E., waves of Indo-European invaders mounted on horses swarmed down from the steppes of what is now Russia, subjugated the peaceful gynocentric cultures, and imposed domination. Gimbutas and the ecofeminists who agree with her argue that these invaders worshipped warrior gods or sky gods and imposed hierarchy on idyllic "Old Europe." The ecofeminist writers see the culture that descended from these so called Kurgan invaders as unremittingly preoccupied with power and domination. Little that happened in Western history after the destruction of Neolithic cultures—in the fourth millennium B.C.E.—is relevant to the present need for ecological reconstruction. For ecofeminist Mara Lynn Keller, the period that lay between the end of "the early epoch of mother-centered life" and the present time was a "long period of patriarchal class rule, a long dark age reaching until this point." Starhawk feels that whereas "western culture is rooted in myths of progress," it more closely resembles "a myth of regress."[3] Despite the presumed invasions, the ethos of the Neolithic matricentric culture is said to have survived in the distant outpost of Minoan Crete before it, too, was destroyed.

For ecofeminists who advance this interpretation of history, we in 1990s Western culture should remember the values of the "golden age" as a part of solving the ecological crisis, since, as Eisler argues, "these ancient societies were structured very much like the more peaceful and just society we are now trying to construct." The rediscovery of these "traditions," which we can "reclaim," she argues, "signals a way out of our alienation from one another and from nature...The reclamation of these traditions can be the basis for the restructuring of society." Spretnak agrees: "Peaceful and progressive societies thrived for millennia where gynocentric values prevailed, for example, in Minoan Crete and Old Europe. In short, we have lived sanely before, we can do it again."[4]

Based on ethnographic analogy, early Neolithic horticultural societies in fact are likely to have been fairly gender-egalitarian. Lying at the heart of these societies was the largely female domestic realm, as Murray Bookchin has pointed out, in relation to which the political realm had barely been differentiated. As such, the private realm was essentially the only social realm in these communities, and women would have had considerable prominence.[5] In horticultural societies generally, the status of women is regularly higher than it is in so-called civilized societies, and there is much greater social equality between women and men than is typical of, for example, oxen-and-plow agriculturalists.

Ethnographic parallels beyond Gimbutas' researches also support ecofeminist claims that early Neolithic societies were relatively egalitarian and matricentric. Some early Neolithic cultures, like the Linear Pottery Culture (5500-4800 B.C.E.) in Czechoslovakia had longhouses, like the Iroquois of North America. Longhouses are often associated with matrilocality and matrilineality. Among the matrilineal and matrilocal Iroquois, as anthropologist Eleanor Leacock has noted,

> the women of the longhouse controlled the distribution of the food and other stores that made up the wealth of the group; they nominated and could depose the sachems or chiefs that represented each tribe in the Council of the Confederacy; and they "had a a voice upon all questions" brought before the clan councils.[6]

Like the Iroquois, the Linear Pottery Culture of the early Neolithic had large rectangular longhouses. Archaeologist Margaret Ehrenberg observes that this suggests a pattern "of matrilocal residence units based on the maternal grandmother and her daughters with their husbands and children." Moreover, the burials of the Linear Pottery Culture, as Ehrenberg writes, "seem to confirm the model of a society where women were not dominated by men." Few goods are found in graves, and those that exist seem to be of equal quality and quantity. The archaeological evidence suggests, she concludes, that women were "highly valued" and "played a leading role in many aspects of life, enjoying status at least equal to that of men."[7]

Moreover, these early Neolithic cultures seem to have been remarkably peaceful. Matrilocal societies generally tend to be, such as these early Neolithic communities are likely to have been, more peaceful than patrilocal societies if only because adult male relatives are dispersed among a number of villages there. "They are therefore less likely to make war on other villages of the same culture," Ehrenberg notes, "as in effect this would involve fighting and killing their own brothers."[8]

While taking into account ecofeminist claims about early neolithic cultures, a few troubling questions do remain that require attention. For one, by the beginning of the Late Neolithic, farmers had displaced the hunter-gatherers and other peoples throughout much of Europe. It is difficult to believe that this was merely a peaceful expansion, particularly since at the western edges of the Linear culture, archaeologists have found more projectiles than in the rest of that Neolithic culture. As archaeologist Sarunas Milisauskas prudently suggests, this question is in need of further investigation by archaeologists.[9] Moreover, problems persist regarding individuality in kinship societies generally, the nature of the moral ethos in kinship societies, the existence of social stratification and ranking, and the role of religious hierarchies, all of which we shall examine presently.

That "gylanic" cultures were as "caring" as these ecofeminists claim, however, is questionable. There is disquieting evidence of human sacrifice in these early cultures. Gimbutas herself noted that infant graves at the Neolithic site of Obre, Yugoslavia, suggest "a ritual offering of small children," and sites at Karanova (in Bulgaria) may show evidence of "dedicatory sacrifice." At Vinca, "human sacrifice accompanied by animal sacrifice was performed in open-air sanctuaries." And the Tartaria tablets, sometimes thought to indicate that Vinca had writing, "were found in association with scorched human bones, twenty-six schematic Early Vinca clay figurines...in an ash-filled sacrificial pit located in the lowest layer of the site."[10] Thus, even if early Neolithic societies were benign in some respects, this does not exclude a whole host of other problems.

The Neolithic "Goddess"

Although there are social reasons why early Neolithic cultures are likely to have been peaceful and egalitarian and even matricentric, ecofeminists are regrettably less interested in the social reasons for these traits than in religious ones. They prefer to explain these benign features by a single supposition: that these cultures worshipped a goddess. The peacefulness and gender-equality and respect for nature of Neolithic cultures can thus be "reclaimed" if we once again "reaffirm our ancient covenant, our sacred bond with our mother the Goddess of nature and spirituality."[11] Worship of the goddess is apparently the magic carpet by which we can reclaim the "women's values" of the Neolithic.

Was a goddess or a diversity of goddesses worshipped in prehistoric Europe? It should be noted that archaeologist Gimbutas simply *assumed* that the female figurines from the early Neolithic in Eastern Europe were consistently goddesses. She offered no reasons for this interpretation, but merely asserted it, as if it were self-evident. Many would agree with her, but other archaeologists are critical of the narrowly *religious* interpretation Gimbutas made of her material, calling her "not very good in critical analysis," "leaping...to conclusions without any intervening argument." Says Neolithic archaeologist Ruth Tringham, "No other archaeologist I know would express this certainty" about the existence of the goddess and its presumed social consequences.[12]

Ironically, Gimbutas believes that her figurines represent air and water divinities, not earth goddesses, as her ecofeminist followers believe. Surprisingly indeed, worship of these air and water divinities, writes Gimbutas, stood "in contrast to the Indo-Europeans, to whom Earth was the Great Mother." Worship of a goddess who specifically represents the earth is thus for Gimbutas characteristic not of the early Neolithic societies of "Old Europe" but of the Indo-European peoples who allegedly destroyed their culture. Insofar as Gimbutas writes of a great goddess, "a supreme Creator who creates from her own substance," this goddess is to be "*contrast[ed]* with the Indo-European Earth-Mother."(emphasis added)[13]

Certainly, the worship of a goddess of some kind is very probable for Neolithic Çatal Hüyük, where fertility cults and a Mother Goddess are historically attested for later periods. Here, female figurines are found sometimes tucked in brickwork, and sometimes in shrines. But if it is reasonable to assert that a goddess of some kind was worshipped in this Neolithic village, can the same explanation be given for *all* the figurines found for the Paleolithic and Neolithic? The Paleolithic and Neolithic are very long periods of time and include a great variety of cultures. Women's status and functions almost certainly varied a great deal over these periods. This makes it very difficult to generalize about the meaning of the figurines in various cultures, as well as their relationship to the status of women.[14]

To be sure, at least some of the full-figured female figurines do seem to have represented a goddess or a fertility principle of some kind in the early Neolithic, as Bookchin himself asserts in *The Ecology of Freedom*.[15] Let us agree that a Great Mother Goddess or a diversity of goddesses were worshipped in some way in these prehistoric European cultures. It is highly plausible that a generative female principle of some kind was indeed revered and it is likely that her function in early cultures would have been to explain the origins of things, of both the cosmos and of human beings, especially before the role of males in impregnation was understood. Paleolithic and early Neolithic might well have drawn a close analogy between women's bearing of children and this female generative principle's "bearing" of the cosmos. That the word "mother goddess" can be applied to such a generative principle in the early Neolithic is reasonable.

But we cannot simply ignore a troubling aspect of an all-embracing goddess interpretation of *all* these figurines, namely that a great many of them were found not in shrines, as at Çatal Hüyük, but in home sites, in piles of debris, along with flint tools and other refuse. For example, the well-known Dolni Vestonice figurine was found not in a shrine but among domestic debris.[16] This hardly suggests that such figures necessarily represent a goddess, in the sense that we use that word today, for it is not likely that worshippers of a goddess would have put her image in the trash.

One possible explanation accounting for these figurines found in debris is that they were used in sympathetic magic. Their exaggerated sexual characteristics suggest that they may have had personal fertility uses, as "part of sympathetic magic rituals aimed at making individual women pregnant," as Ehrenberg suggests. The use of figurines for this purpose "may have been perceived as even more important in societies where the link between male impregnation and childbirth was not fully understood."

> A woman wishing for a child would make, or have made, a model either of herself pregnant, or—more commonly in known ethnographic examples—of the hoped-for child, perhaps shown as the adult they would eventually become. She might then carry the image around, perhaps sleep alongside it, or use it to perform other rituals.

After the hoped-for child was born, the mother may have simply thrown the figurine away, it having served its purpose. The fact that many of the Paleolithic and early Neolithic figurines were often among debris strengthens this interpretation, for the image could easily have been discarded after the woman became pregnant. As Ehrenberg observes, ethnographic analogy provides support for this interpretation.

> Amongst several North-American Indian tribes, such as the Zuni, a woman wanting a baby carries a model around, keeps it in a cradle, or places it

on an altar until she becomes pregnant. After the
successful birth of a child the model is in some
cases thrown away and in others carefully kept
by the mother to ensure the child's future
prosperity.[17]

I am not trying to cast aside the notion that the worship of a
Great Goddess or Mother Goddess was widespread in prehistory,
but I am concerned to show that every figurine does not a goddess
make, particularly in cultures that worship a fertility principle. Nor
was every culture that worshipped a goddess necessarily—indeed,
inexorably—benign.

The Mystique of Minoan Crete

Perhaps the best example of this can be found in a much later
society that many ecofeminists celebrate—Minoan Crete. This
Bronze Age culture ranks high among some ecofeminists as a
favorite site for paradise, epitomizing the sensuous, free, peaceful,
gender-equal, nature-loving society, complete with priestesses,
goddesses, and perhaps even a queen. "Clearly the goddess was
supreme," trumpets Merlin Stone in her famous book on goddess
religion, echoed by Eisler and others who are in the spell of the
Neolithic mystique. The array of depictions of women in frescoes,
the discovery of "snake goddesses," and the finding of the "queen's
megaron" in the palace of Knossos are presumed to support this
alluring portrait.

Alas, archaeological support for the existence of a queen in
Minoan Crete is highly precarious indeed. Sir Arthur Evans, the
excavator of the palace of Knossos on whose work this mystique is
largely built, almost arbitrarily chose a certain room in the palace
to be "the queen's megaron" or bedroom—although, as Sarah
Pomeroy dryly observes, "this room was not found with a label on
it."[18] Evans's reason for making this dubious judgment was that a
certain seat—presumably a throne—in the room *was found to be
somewhat lower and wider than the others.* For the Victorian Evans
(who regarded women as obstructions during his excavation), this

was sufficient evidence to show that the seat was designed for a female. His label for the room as "the queen's megaron," as Pomeroy points out, has stuck and has ever since been published and republished, with no indication that this attribution was without any archaeological foundation whatever. There is actually no evidence that this room belonged to a queen, or a king, or even a monarch of any kind.

The fact is that architectural evidence simply cannot supply ironclad information about gender relations. We cannot even be sure that the people who lived in the Bronze Age building at Knossos were monarchs at all. Recently, historian Rodney Castleden has convincingly argued that the structure at Knossos is far less likely to have been a royal palace—as most people who consider the question have often unthinkingly assumed, following "the fruit of Sir Arthur Evans' imagination" (as Castleden puts it)—than a temple. Many goddesses were worshipped in the Knossos temple, Castleden argues, both in public rituals and in esoteric ceremonies for initiates in secluded sanctuaries. Among these goddesses was the Great Goddess Potnia, who was familiar throughout the Mycenaean world. The worship of the Minoan goddesses involved intoxication and ritual ecstatic dancing.[19]

Castleden believes that the elite women of this temple—the priestesses—had very high status, even acting as epiphanies of the goddesses in ceremonies. This priestesshood was "highly organized," he writes, and the priestess inhabitants of the temple would have been quite wealthy, since the many storerooms in the structure indicate that it was unquestionably a depot for revenue, "gathered in either as voluntary offerings to the temple and its deities or as compulsory taxes." Like Sumerian temples (which also housed priestesses), the Knossos labyrinth may well have functioned "as the dwelling-place of deities, as a ceremonial centre and a centre for worship, as a treasury and storehouse and as a commercial and manufacturing centre. In addition it housed the priests, priestesses and temple workers." The king himself—if there was one—may have relied on the priestesses for his wealth and position, and for divine approval of his reign.[20] Yet it must be noted that even if women did have high status in Minoan temples as priestesses, this does not reflect on the lives of ordinary women. All the "evidence" for Crete as an ecofeminist paradise comes from the buildings of the elite strata. The Minoan temple enclave represented, in fact, an elite with wealth, status, and religious sanctification—in no way different from the hierarchial priestly corporations that exploited many portions of Mesopotamia and ancient Egypt.

The existence of social stratification at Crete, however, disturbs ecofeminist theists not in the least. Nor do the other ways in which the culture apparently hardened its heart, for it is not at all clear that the ethos of Minoan Crete reflected women's presumably "life-loving" values. A recent excavation at Knossos by the British School at Athens led by Peter Warren found concrete evidence pointing to ritualistic child sacrifice in Minoan Crete, despite the existence of priestesses and goddess worship. Each of almost three hundred bones that came from two children and were found in a pithos (or storage jar) had certain cut marks in them, not at the joints but in midbone, which, as Warren says, are

> clear evidence that their flesh was carefully cut away, much in the manner of the flesh of sacrificed animals. In fact, the bones of a slaughtered sheep were found with those of the children....Moreover, as far as the bones are concerned, the children appear to have been in good health....Startling as it may seem, the available evidence so far points to an argument that the children were slaughtered and their flesh cooked and possibly eaten in a sacrificial ritual made in the service of a nature deity to assure the annual renewal of fertility.[21]

Warren was by no means looking for such evidence about Crete. If anything, he was astonished by what he found. Castleden, for his part, criticizes Warren for his conservative belief "that human sacrifice was rare and exceptional in Minoan culture" and argues that the conclusion that "human sacrifice was an integral part of the Minoan belief-system" seems "inescapable." At a sanctuary near Knossos, Castleden notes, "were found the remains of a 17-year-old youth."

> His ankles had evidently been tied and his legs folded up to make him fit onto the table....He had been ritually murdered with the long bronze dagger engraved with a boar's head that lay beside him.[22]

It is unlikely that this socially stratified and even cruel society can be said to constitute a matricentric paradise. If Knossos was a temple complex for the worship of goddesses, as Castleden argues, its supposedly "caring and nurturing" ethos was not such that it discouraged such horrors. Minoan Crete was a Bronze Age civilization, and it would defy archaeological credibility to assume that such a highly developed civilization could have been anything but hierarchical, exploitative, and oppressive.

Philosophical Idealism

This history leads us to a strategic question. It is not the question of whether the early Neolithic cultures of "Old Europe" were peaceful, matricentric, and gender-egalitarian—they probably were. The question is not even whether they worshipped an immanent or transcendent female deity. There is every reason to suspect that a female generative principle that can be called a Mother Goddess was revered in Neolithic cultures, especially for purposes of fertility. Rather, the question that must be raised is that of the *relationship* of that goddess to the many social factors that enter into shaping an early community. Did the worship of a goddess orchestrate early social relations? Or did the social relations in the cultures themselves produce the goddess?

This is a profoundly important issue that reveals one of ecofeminism's greatest failings. A number of ecofeminists clearly appear to believe that merely by changing the content of myths from "bad ones" to "good ones"—such as by worshiping a goddess instead of a god—we somehow change the key social realities of

our lives. They would agree with Lynn White's very naive judgment that "[s]ince the roots of our trouble are so largely religious,
the remedy must also be essentially religious, whether we call it
that or not." Riane Eisler, for example, is seeking "the 'critical mass'
of new images and myths that is required for their actualization by
a sufficient number of people."[23] Spretnak seems to feel that changing the sex of a culture's deity yields profound political and social
differences for that culture. A veritable religious determinist in her
version of history, Spretnak seems to believe that culture is shaped
primarily by religion: she identifies "the largest mobilized force
trying to defeat us" as "patriarchal religion." Indeed, for Spretnak,
"[c]oopting and replacing the Goddess" was an act "motivated by
one desperate drive: to prevent woman from experiencing her
power."[24]

That cultural symbols do help legitimate and reinforce social
orders is not in dispute. Ideas play an important role in social
change. But not predictably, not everywhere, not under all circumstances, and not in every way. The anthropological record, for
example, reveals no clear pattern of correspondence between goddess worship and a high social and political status for women. In
fact, in many cases goddess worship may correspond to a low-status
female position. The religion of Burma, Theravada Buddhism, for
example, has no goddess at all. Yet Burmese women have historically had a relatively high status compared with women in most
other cultures, with "a power that is awesome to behold," observes
anthropologist John Ferguson.[25] By contrast, Chinese Buddhism
does have a female deity; in fact, Kwan Yin is probably the most
worshipped and widely depicted deity in Chinese Buddhism. The
ideology of Taoism gives the male and female principles, yang and
yin, equal weight. Yet neither the worship of Kwan Yin nor the
interaction of yin and yang has prevented China from being the
epitome of a patriarchal society. Nor has fervent worship of the
Virgin of Guadalupe—one of the most revered of mother goddesses
and a Mexican national symbol—done much for Mexican women.
That culture, too, is notably patriarchal and notoriously macho.[26]

That patricentric societies worship goddesses shows, if anything, the *weakness* of goddess-worship as a *force* in organizing a

society along non-hierarchical, gender-equal, and peaceful lines. Ecofeminists like Spretnak may note that goddesses have been "co-opted" by men, but they were certainly not "co-opted" at Knossos. We are plunged into a characteristic ecofeminist double bind, where facts are valid if they suit ecofeminist theory and should be ignored if they do not. But social realities make a significant difference as to whether cultural symbols carry weight. Least of all can we say that if we begin worshipping a goddess today, women's situation will thereby improve. To assert that it will is rank philosophical idealism, ignoring the social factors that institutionalize women's oppression.

In any case, a veritable flood of scholars have warned us against seeking one-to-one correspondences between a culture's myths and its social and political realities. According to Marina Warner, "There is no logical equivalence in any society between exalted female objects of worship and a high position for woman." In fact, anthropologist Ena Campbell finds that "[m]other goddess worship seems to stand in *inverse* relationship with high secular female status" (emphasis added). Archaeologist Ehrenberg sees "no obvious correlation between the existence of goddesses and the roles and status of real women, and it is extremely dangerous to use mythology as a source of evidence for history." Eminent feminist classical scholar Sarah Pomeroy concludes, "To use the mother goddess theory to draw any conclusions regarding the high status of human females of the time [prehistory] would be foolhardy...[T]he mother may be worshiped in societies where male dominance and even misogyny are rampant."[27] The relationship between a symbol and a society, as most anthropologists know, is extremely complex, and one cannot make generalizations that link goddess symbolism to the social roles of women.

Social factors—matrilineality, matrilocality, horticulture, the domestic nature of the society—can easily account for the benign features that ecofeminists attribute to the early Neolithic. It is far more likely that goddess worship, where it existed, was itself a product of these social factors than the other way around. To think that we can "reclaim the traditions" of the Neolithic through worshipping a goddess today is absurd.

The Origins of Hierarchy

The emergence of hierarchy, patriarchy, warfare, social inequality, and various religions involves a subtle dialectic that would require an intensive discussion to unravel. Certainly by the time of the earliest written records in the fourth millennium B.C.E., male dominance and other hierarchies had been established. Farming had become primarily a male occupation throughout Europe, and warfare was a hard fact of everyday life. Burials had shifted from the communal to the individual, social ranking had become increasingly stratified, and agriculture had made possible the accumulation of wealth and power.

The archaeological sites in Eastern Europe reveal a clear shift from a relatively pacific to a more warlike and socially stratified society. More weapons are found in the layers from the later Neolithic. Burials of single individuals—in "kurgans," or burial mounds—begin to appear. These are likely to have been burials of individuals of higher status than others, such as chiefs, indicating that hierarchies were already very much in place. The exceptionally rich graves, with silver and gold ornaments, precious stones, and battle-axes, daggers, and knives, moreover, were reserved exclusively for males.

The question is, what happened? What was the origin of patriarchy and other hierarchies? The ecofeminist-theists, following Gimbutas, answer that hierarchy was *imposed* from without by invading pastoral nomads. These "Kurgan invaders" supposedly originated in the Pontic and Volga steppe area around the Black Sea and invaded Neolithic Europe beginning in the fifth millennium B.C.E. For Gimbutas, that there was a series of invasions is self-evident. "It was clear," she wrote, "that only a new force from beyond the Dnieper could have caused the upheaval and disintegration of the long-lasting and flourishing [Neolithic] cultures of Europe and their contemporaries."[28] A warrior culture, whose fighting men rode chariot-type vehicles and and on horseback, the "Kurgans" supposedly conquered the peaceful goddess-worshippers. "Picture yourself," Spretnak breathes,

> as a witness of that decisive moment in history, that is, as a resident of the peaceful, artful, Goddess-oriented culture of Old Europe. ...It is 4500 B.C. You are walking along a high ridge, looking out across the plains to the east. In the distance you see a massive wave of horsemen galloping toward your world on strange, powerful animals.[29]

From that "decisive moment"—which we ourselves can reexperience!—dates patriarchy pure and simple, the regime that has since led directly to the present-day ecodisaster. The invaders "brought a sky god, a warrior cult, and patriarchal social order. They formed a ruling class over the old village goddess-worshipping culture," says Spretnak, "*and that is where we live today*—in an Indo-European culture." Moreover, in conquering the goddess cultures they essentially "desacralized the earth" by worshipping sky gods.[30] So much for all literary, philosophical, technical, musical, artistic, and cultural achievements of the millennia between the disappearance of the idyllic Neolithic and the modern era. Ironically, even a passing reading of Western philosophy will show that "post-Kurgan" times were resplendent with richly endowed organismic philosophies and cosmologies, indeed, that a "mechanized worldview" was a very recent phenomenon.

But did hierarchy solely originate with such invasions? Although some theorists—typically, Joseph Campbell and Ashley Montagu—support Gimbutas' theory, it would be dodging the question to attribute the origins of hierarchy simply to invasions. The story itself seems very doubtful. For one thing, the shift in artifacts apparent at Eastern European archaeological sites need not have resulted from an invasion at all. It can more easily be attributed to an *internal* development of hierarchy, as would be the case with the increasing pre-eminence of male economic and political power over women. For another, there is no evidence for a shift from an agricultural to a pastoral social order in the period in question. "No significant differences in the types of plants and animals exploited are observed in comparing the Middle Neolithic farming societies [after the alleged "invasions" began] with their Early Neolithic predecessors in most areas of Europe," archaeologist Milisauskas writes. "The traditional picture of groups of pure pastoralists displacing groups of pure farmers represents a naive oversimplification."[31]

Nor is it' clear what would have caused the "Kurgans" to migrate westward in the first place. In later times, to be sure, "pressure from one set of pastoralists on another often triggered a chain reaction of migrations that eventually affected Europe," as Milisauskas notes. In the first millennium B.C.E., for example, the Scythians, Sarmatians, and Cimmerians attacked European and Near Eastern state societies probably as a result of population pressure and/or warfare in their area. But it is not likely that these would have been motivating forces in the relatively quiescent middle Neolithic.[32] Archaeologist Colin Renfew, who discreetly calls Gimbutas' archaeology "not convincing," also disputes the invasion theory on several compelling grounds. "Perhaps the strongest objection is simply the lack of conviction behind the whole story," he writes. "Why on earth should hordes of mounted warriors have moved west at the end of the Neolithic, subjugating the inhabitants of Europe and imposing the proto-Indo-European language on them? What enormous upsurge of population on the Steppes could have been responsible?" To cast even greater doubt on the invasion theory, it is not even clear that residents of the steppes at that time rode horses in battle at all! "The supposed military advantage of the Kurgan warriors (the fact that they were mounted) is hypothetical, since it is not clear that there were mounted warriors at the time."[33]

Other holes appear in this highly simplistic story that deserve attention. Çatal Hüyük, like other Anatolian sites, disappeared long *before* the "Kurgan invasions" are said to have begun. Nor does the "Kurgan invasion" theory explain how the Kurgans *themselves* developed hierarchy, as Elizabeth Fox-Genovese pointed out in her *New York Times* review of Eisler's book. The Kurgans' presumed hierarchical social order, after all, must have come from somewhere. Were they invaded too? The "Kurgan invasion" theory is what we might call an "asteroid theory" of hierarchy, for it explains its emergence literally by means of a *deus ex machina*. Finally, the "Kurgan invasion" theory does not explain the origin of hierarchy in non-Western cultures. The Chinese and the Aztecs, for example, developed hierarchy, centralized states, warfare, and male deities with no help whatsoever from either Indo-European invaders or Spretnak's fertile imagination.

Although invasions of various sorts doubtless play a role in the development of some cultures' hierarchies, the emergence of hierarchy as such must also be examined as a process of *internal* development, from internal social tensions that led to the emergence of status groups within many communities themselves, resulting in the gradual development of political and class elites, as well as religious and gender ones. Generally, the ethnography of present-day tribal societies describes an evolution from the egalitarianism of band hunting-gathering societies, to the status differentiations and ranking of tribal societies, to the shamans and priesthoods of simple and complex chiefdoms and warrior societies. By ethnographic analogy, this course of development is likely to have occurred in Neolithic Europe as well, without the assistance of invading patriarchal horsemen who may or may not have had horses.

Neolithic Eastern Europe itself provides us with considerable evidence for the theory that hierarchy emerged from within communities, not from external invasions. Just to the north of Vinca, sites for the Linear culture suggests the emergence of gerontocracy: the burials indicate "status differences [that] were based primarily on age and sex. Spondylus shells and other artifacts made of nonlocal raw material are strongly associated with old males."[34] What Gimbutas sees as rich "Kurgan" burials, notes Renfrew, "many archaeologists see...as essentially local phenomena in which prestige goods were buried with members of emerging aristocracies."[35] Neolithic Malta, too, was a chiefdom society and had developed around a complex of organized priesthoods and temples on the island, apparently without disruption from pastoral nomads.[36]

Many theories have been proposed that trace an historical, dialectical development of stratification over a fairly long expanse of time without recourse to the *deus ex machina* of invading warriors. Marxist anthropologists have often recounted the rise of wealth and class societies to explain domination. Eleanor Leacock, for example, cites a progression from sharing to barter to wealth, exchange, and vested interests:

> A profoundly social process—sharing—sparked the change, for sharing developed into barter, which in turn developed into the systematic trade and specialization of labor that eventually led to the innovation of individually held wealth and power....In the course of human history, the increasingly stable village life...called for more and more regularized exchange both within and among groups. In turn, specialization became common in the production of goods to be traded for luxury items and special tools and foods.[37]

For Leacock, patriarchy and class differences arose simultaneously. Murray Bookchin, while noting that invasions did play a significant role for various societies, many of which were already stratified, traces a complex development of hierarchy through forms from within the structure of preliterate societies, beginning with gerontocracy.

> Where settled agricultural communities were invaded by pastoral nomads, the shift from one social arena to another may have occurred so explosively that it acquired apocalyptic proportions....But such sweeping changes were rare. More often than not, past and present were subtly melded together into a striking variety of social forms. In such cases, we witness a slow assimilation of traditional forms to new ends, a repeated use of old relationships for new purposes.[38]

Bookchin traces the development of hierarchy in early societies dialectically, even as exchange, wealth, and class society
developed. He shows how various aspects of organic society were
transformed into hierarchies: how age differences developed into
gerontocracies, how a separate "sexual division of culture" became
gender hierarchy, how shamans developed into priesthoods, and
how powerless "chiefs" whose status was derived from their ability
to disperse "gifts" were transformed into powerful chiefs. Above
all, he emphasizes the emergence of the political or public realm
out of the private, domestic world of societies like those of the early
Neolithic, a political realm whose impulses included a cooperative
egalitarian impulse to combat hierarchies based on ranking and
wealth—as well as a political realm of warriors and developing
hierarchy.[39] The ecofeminist reduction of the origin of hierarchy
solely to "invasions," then, is simplistic in the extreme, as is the
Neolithic mystique generally. Explanation of hierarchy requires a
much more careful examination and a more graded development
than one that elevates all female figurines to goddesses, ignores the
implications of the fact that goddesses were paramount in patricentric and patriarchal societies, dismisses complex transitions in
social structures and values with inexplicable invasions, and
evokes myths that are more characteristic of Disneyland exhibi-
tions than authentic folk traditions.

The Myth of Primary Oppression

To be sure, not all ecofeminists agree with Spretnak, Eisler,
and others that hierarchy resulted from invasion. But as we have
seen, many accept the idea that the oppression of women constitutes the primary oppression in society today. Ynestra King, for
example, with her background in social ecology, agrees that hierarchy developed from within, but she differs with social ecology in
arguing that the subordination of women, not gerontocracy, was the
earliest form of domination. She "starts with the assumption that
the original form of domination in human society and therefore the
prototype of all other forms of domination, was that of men over

women."[40] Indeed, no matter what ecofeminists regard as the proximate cause of environmental dislocations—the Scientific Revolution, Christianity, the classical Greeks, the "Kurgans"—for most, the ultimate and continuing cause is patriarchy and the oppression of women.

It should be emphasized here that although women's subordination in the West began very early in prehistory—indeed, that it is "prototypical," to use King's term or "archetypal," to use Bookchin's—it is a quantum leap to reduce all hierarchy to patriarchy. Hierarchy and domination were elaborated into many different forms and often extended in directions that did not necessarily challenge the status of women. Organized societies of warriors are not excluded even in societies where women have a high social status. For example, although Iroquois women held positions of great status and the culture was not pitted against nonhuman nature, Iroquois warriors were notoriously ferocious and conducted expansionist wars. Other kinds of hierarchy have coexisted with a high degree of gender equality as well, oppressing both women and men with perfect equanimity. For example, women and nature were very highly valued in ancient Egypt, as Barbara Lesko points out. Egyptian women "enjoyed equal legal rights with men. Considered as fully adult and responsible for their own acts, they inherited and disposed of property as free agents, just as they gave testimony in court or entered into business contracts on their own with no male cosignatory needed." Nevertheless, Egypt was extremely hierarchical, structured around the pharoah, vast theocracy, and later a caste system. "Egyptians apparently did not characterize women as the 'weaker sex,' Lesko says, "so women could be called up by the state for labor service, apparently as part of the tax program." During the Middle Kingdom, women were subject to corvée labor, like men. Here, both sexes were "equally" degraded under an autocratic system of tyranny and domination."[41] If we are to accept Herodotus' account, Egyptian women even enjoyed high status in the family structure of ordinary peasants as well.

The highly selective approach toward data that ecofeminists exhibit is also reflected in their capacity to overlook the role of priestesses as well as priests in the evolution of early hierarchies. In Starhawk's account of the emergence of hierarchy in Sumer, for example, the important role of priesthoods is all but ignored. Indeed, priestesses—as distinguished from priests—somehow seem to be an acceptable form of hierarchy to ecofeminist-theists.[42] They seem to mistake the purported egalitarianism in goddess worship for an absence of religious hierarchy. A goddess is primarly a cultural symbol; a priesthood is the real thing—a genuine institutional hierarchy, whatever may be the sex of the priest or priestess and however egalitarian may be the symbol they seem to promote. Indeed, the very word *hierarchy* is etymologically derived from the Greek word for "priest"—and, for that matter, "priestess."

Even the ecofeminist-theists' own sources reveal that goddess worship was probably often mediated by priestesses—that is to say, religious hierarchies. Minoan Crete, as we have seen, may well have been ruled by an organized priestesshood. Neolithic Çatal Hüyük, too, is believed to have contained an organized class of priests and priestesses. There, opines Mellaart, "the cult of the goddess was administered mainly by women."[43] Matricentric Vinca itself was apparently a very ceremonial culture, as Renfrew has pointed out; the heavy stylization of the figurines, the clothing, the masks—all suggest a highly developed religious culture.[44] If Renfrew's suggestions are to be accepted, we would be obliged to suppose that such stylization was the product of a hierarchical religious structure that, while it may have included women, would have been based on a system of command and obedience. Implicit in the ecofeminist accolades to Mellaart's writings is the hidden assumption that if women participate in a hierarchy it is good, but if men do so it is bad.

But there is no reason to think that temples run by priestesses for a goddess or goddesses were less authoritarian and power-oriented than temples run by men for gods. In the Neolithic and Chalcolithic eras, writes Merlin Stone rather unabashedly, "temples of the Goddess...appear to have been the core of the community, apparently owning the land, the herds of animals and most material property."[45] Similarly, in ancient Sumer and perhaps at

Knossos, temples often became centers for the storage and distribution of food surpluses by commanding priestly elites, a power that enhanced mightily the authority of temples—over which presided priests and priestesses alike.

We should also be alert to the fact that a society imbued with such familial, presumably "maternal" sentiments as "caring" may not have extended that "caring" to human beings of diverse ethnic origins—or, for that matter, to the natural world. There is no reason to believe that the love that a mother extends to children and to other members of her family would have been able to resist the problems raised by the pressure of population growth, climatic changes that altered the food supply, or the impact of natural disasters. The evidence of human sacrifice already constitutes disturbing evidence of barbarities that, according to ecofeminist-theists, should have been completely alien to the all-caring, all-loving, and benign goddess of idyllic matricentric communities. In any case, the speculation that the ills of the world result exclusively from a shift from a matricentric to a warrior society can be matched, if we choose to do so, by the speculation that internal developments of hierarchy in a strictly matricentric culture are likely to have produced them.

"Prototypical" or "archetypal" as the oppression of women may be, the claim that it underpins *all* later forms of oppression in society is even more difficult to substantiate today, when one scans the complex systems of oppression that afflict the entire landscape of society. To be sure, no thinking person will seriously disagree that the liberation of women from the gender roles to which they have been confined holds the promise of liberating men from gender roles as well. Shedding roles that require males to be breadwinners or to suppress tender feelings would certainly be emancipatory for them. It is true that, despite the obvious privileges that male domination gives men, gender roles also confine males to stereotypical roles of their own, and this keeps them from exercising the full range of their human capacities for love, cooperativeness, trust, and a nurturing emotional life in general. In these senses, feminism promises liberation for men as well as women.

But it is difficult to see how freeing women from misogyny will also free women—or men—from oppression under capitalism and the nation-state, let alone from racist societies. Even as they dominate women, men dominate other men in their own right, *and they do this not for the ultimate purpose of dominating women* but for very clear reasons that require no psychoanalysis to explain. Men do not become capitalists because they are misogynists or emotionally repressed, or because they are afraid of women's "elemental power." Their aims, reasons, motivations, and methods are much more mundane, as a careful reading of any economic text will reveal. They usually stand to gain very distinct things, such as material wealth, status, vast state power, and military control—things that some women, too, have not been immune to wanting. Nazis wanted to kill Jews, homosexuals, and gypsies, but not women as such; they used German women for their own purposes and even "glorified" them in pursuit of their ends. We need not mystify this by attributing to male capitalists, for example, unprovable and inferred gender-derived neuroses. What they stand to gain is clear.

Systems of domination like capitalism, statism, and ethnic oppressions—and sexism itself—have a "history, logic, and struggle" of their own, as Susan Prentice, a critic of ecofeminism, puts it. They are conscious projects in their own right. While the ecofeminist view that the domination of women is prototypical may be sound, it cannot be used to supplant the elaboration of domination into all different spheres of social life. "By locating the origin of the domination of women and nature in male consciousness," writes Prentice, "ecofeminism makes political and economic systems simply derivative of male thinking."[46]

The state, for example, a very late development in the emergence of hierarchies, classes, and even quasi-state formations, appeared as the institution that acquired the legal monopoly of violence and as such was the instrument of ruling classes par excellence for dominating *all* subjugated people, men and women alike, not to mention people of color. To simplistically trace the emergence of the state directly to the oppression of women by men is not only reductionist but reveals an appalling ignorance of the extremely complex class as well as hierarchical mediations that gave rise to it in all its different historical forms. Ecofeminism would stand at odds with a whole body of radical theory to claim that the state has its origins in the family and more specifically in the attempt to dominate women. One would have to assume that such disparate antistatist thinkers as Rosa Luxemburg and Emma Goldman were basically wrong when they viewed the state as a sine qua non for the existence of class society—a later development than and product of a purely hierarchical society. Parallels (like Robert Filmer's in the 17th century) between the state and the family—which was already regarded as a "natural" and good institution—were retrospective attempts to legitimate the state more than they were models consciously or unconsciously followed to construct it. If any previous institution is likely to have served as a clear-cut model for the state, it was early military systems of command-and-obedience, like those that existed in warrior strata—based on an oppression of men by men. Military forms of organization are much more clearly the model for the emergence of the state than the domination of women. In the early modern period, justifications for the "divine right" of monarchy and the sovereignty of monarchical rule had a clear model in the papal sovereignty of the Middle Ages.

Nor did capitalism emerge in order to control or dominate women. Seeking profit, to put it mildly, was a more compelling motive. Prentice argues, against ecofeminism, that

> there is an internal logic to capitalism—for example, its relations and forces of production, commodity fetishism, exploitation, domination, alienation, etc.—that makes exploiting nature a sensible thing for capitalism as a world-system to do. It is no mere failure or stunting of consciousness: it is consciousness directed and organized for a different end.[47]

That particular end has little direct connection with the relations between the sexes.

Racism can be said to have had its roots in the in-group folk parochialisms of tribal society generally, which led to ethnic chauvinisms that have been part of the human experience from ancient times onward. It is generally agreed in the ethnographic literature that tribal societies were highly exclusive, and cultures of the early Neolithic are unlikely to have been an exception. Tribal groups usually regarded themselves as "the people," in contrast to human beings outside the community. Apart from needed alliances that were mediated by the exchange of goods and the formation of trading partners, everyone who was outside the tribal group was seen as a stranger and was subject to very arbitrary treatment. The classical Greeks were no less guilty of ethnic chauvinism than other peoples in their time, and they participated in the institution of slavery that was a nearly ubiquitous phenomenon for millennia. It was the concept of a generalized *humanitas* that made possible the recognition of a common humanity that cut across ethnic boundaries, a concept that has yet to be fulfilled because of religious chauvinisms, status hierarchies, bureaucracies, and economic factors. European and American slavery was instituted for clearly recognizable purposes of economic gain, as was European imperialism. Over the course of history, societies structured around tribes have been absorbed into those structured around nation-states, and nationalistic and internationalistic hatreds are once again on the rise, as in Eastern Europe today. "Prototypical" or "archetypal" as the domination of women may be, as a model for hierarchy as such, this was by no means the exclusive source of the various forms of hierarchy that were to follow in its wake. Nor need they necessarily disappear with the liberation of women from sexism today.

The present Western ideology of dominating nonhuman nature has distant roots in the history of humanity itself. Indeed, human beings of whatever culture must use nonhuman nature instrumentally for their survival to some extent or other. Like all organisms, human beings must interact with their environment. In some non-Western cultures, like that of the Incas, hierarchy developed without an accompanying ideology of dominating nature, but in the West the idea that humans are separated from and must dominate nonhuman nature has deep roots, accompanying the rise of social hierarchies as such. As early as Hebrew scripture, the idea of dominating nature began to emerge and develop as a God-given calling in the human condition. The evolution in which nonhuman nature was seen as increasingly useful to human beings was fed by the various forms of hierarchy that developed in the West. The emergence of modern systems of domination drew on these earlier roots but set up an even sharper contrast between the human and the nonhuman that was cast in oppositional terms. Capitalism, with its competitive grow-or-die economy, was obliged to exacerbate this ideology of dominating nature, with fearful results for the entire biosphere. Attempts to reduce the ideology of dominating nature exclusively to the domination of women by men serves to obscure the complex relationship between nature and society that has emerged.

But although statism, capitalism, racism, and the attempt to dominate nonhuman nature arose for purposes other than to dominate women, state and capitalist societies have affected women's lives much for the worse. In Mesopotamia, for example, women's status fell—as did that of most men—as monarchies and despotisms consolidated and militarized themselves. The bureaucratization and centralization of nation-states in the eighteenth and nineteenth centuries reduced the amount of control that *everyone* had in their lives at the local level. As the loci of power became more and more remote from the community as a whole, women— less mobile than men because relegated to domestic life—became increasingly marginal to political life. The instrumentalization of social life, the loss of meaningful systems of ethics in favor of utilitarianism—these developments impoverished and brutalized women's lives as well as men's.

Capitalism as an economic phenomenon also affected most women's lives for the worse, as it did the lives of the men who dominated them. It separated the workplace from the home, and it fragmented the domestic sphere into isolated family units. Even for a man or woman with the best will in the world it is almost impossible to spend most of each day and each week working away from home and still be more than a remote figure to children. This completed the process of isolating women—as well as most men—

from the public realm and from each other and rendered them powerless in the political sphere. It eroded the community life on which home manufacturing had previously depended, a life in which women had been highly visible and no less central than men. Today, the recent trends toward increasing hate crimes—violence against women, gay-bashing, anti-Semitism, and racism—could not happen without the extraordinarily pervasive market economy of our own day and its elimination of community and a meaningful existence, not to speak of the extreme poverty of many urban blacks, and the mass-media culture that arouses hate-filled frenzies. Racism and the destruction of the biosphere damage males and females alike. The liberation of women therefore depends on the destruction of these institutions as a whole, not only on the destruction of male domination.

It must be emphasized that all these forms of domination are interrelated, and the firmest, clearest commonality transcending their singularity is the fact that they are all forms of hierarchy. It is only the abolition of hierarchy as such, not of specific hierarchies which have been elaborated from one form of hierarchy into another—patterned as they were on the domination of women by men—that will create the basis of a free society. It is this that social ecology has long advocated. For Ynestra King to write that before ecofeminism, "all hitherto existing philosophies of liberation, with the possible exception of some forms of social anarchism, accept the anthropocentric notion that humanity should dominate nature and that the increasing domination of nonhuman nature is a precondition for true human freedom"[48] is presumptuous as well as misleading. Indeed, the challenge to rule in all its forms posed by social ecology—a "form of social anarchism"—makes it a more radical and all-encompassing outlook than any outlook based on a reductionist attempt to ascribe all hierarchy exclusively to the domination of women by men.

Lacking the political bite of a specific opposition to capitalism and the nation-state, ecofeminism has largely become an exercise in personal transformation. Lacking an understanding of the role of priests and shamans in the development of hierarchy, it has largely become a religion in its own right, with a tendency to breed its own shamanesses and priestesses. Lacking an understanding of the dialectic of several millennia of Western culture, it has become largely atavistic. Lacking a historical understanding of the changing place of women in Western culture, it leaves their self-definition dependent on stereotyped eternal "images" of women, when not on biology itself.

Without a more thorough and dialectically graded analysis of hierarchy than ecofeminism offers, we are left to dismiss most of what happened in Western history since the end of the Neolithic as irrelevant to present concerns. In effect, ecofeminists who have a partiality for the Neolithic write off the long Western revolutionary tradition—not to speak of the Left generally—from historical importance. Certainly the traditional Left has often failed to give sufficient importance to the sensuous and to sensibility, and certainly this failing has to be drastically remedied, but it is no alternative to reduce Western social development to a "myth of regress" after the Neolithic.

Chapter 3

Divine Immanence and the

"Aliveness" of Nature

The very ancient idea that the earth or nature as a whole is a single living organism has been revived in full bloom in ecological discussion recently, and many ecofeminists have been all too ready to adopt it as a basis for a new ecological ethics. Historically, "aliveness" as a cosmology is called *hylozoism,* and it is often assumed that an ethics based on hylozoism would encourage us to value life and would countervail the prevalant trend to destroy the biosphere. Among theistic ecofeminists—albeit not among them alone—the idea of the "aliveness" of nature is closely related to the notion of the "immanence" of the goddess in nature. Starhawk propounds the view that "this Earth is alive and...we are part of her being." If we believe in an immanent goddess, we will understand that nature is alive, and this will help us gain a rich sense of the "immanent value" of life. For Riane Eisler, hylozoism is part of the ethos of the prehistoric societies she loves: there, "the world was viewed as the great Mother, a living entity who in both her temporal and spiritual manifestations creates and nurtures all forms of life."[1]

Hylozoism, we are told, even leads to political activism. "When we understand that the Earth is alive," Starhawk tells us, "she calls us to act to preserve her life." And "when we understand...that the cosmos is alive, then we also understand that everything is interconnected. Just as in our bodies: what happens to a finger affects what happens to a toe." Finally, "when we understand that everything is interconnected, we are called to a politics and a set of actions that come from compassion, from the ability to literally feel with all living beings on earth." Moreover, hylozoism and "interconnectedness," according to Starhawk, even have uniquely anti-capitalist implications. "If we saw ourselves as interconnected parts of the living being that is the Earth, of equal existential value," she writes, "we could no longer justify economic exploitation."[2] Given this alluring ensemble of ideas, hylozoism thus becomes not only an approach for viewing our interconnectedness with natural ecosystems and the inorganic world but a universal panacea for dealing with the problems created by capitalism and social oppression. One may reasonably wonder whether a hylozoistic cosmology would have these political consequences, but one thing remains clear: it has become very popular among a very broad range of ecofeminist theorists.

The Ethics of Divine Immanence

Indeed, not only does a belief in a living immanent deity promote activism, we are told, but religions with transcendental gods have exactly the opposite effect. Starhawk makes the remarkable statement that "spirituality promotes passivity when the domain of spirit is defined as outside the world."[3] One might reasonably object that liberation theology is based on that notoriously dualistic religion called Christianity, but Starhawk knowingly assures us that Latin American peoples who use it *really* regard the Christian divinity as immanent, not transcendent. Precisely where Starhawk has acquired this privileged information remains a mystery. In fact, for Starhawk the issue of divine immanence is so fundamental to political activism that it is beyond discussion, and she tries to eliminate any criticism of that view on the part of people who are white. "The spiritual/political split," we are told, "is a problem of white people." Nor, apparently, can any white citizen of a Western culture question the relevance of immanence theology (or what she calls "spirituality") to political activism, for she dismisses "the debate about the linking of the spiritual and the political" as a form of "cultural imperialism [that] is itself a form of racism."[4] This spectacular instance of baiting those who raise challenging questions about her ideas on the basis of their ethnic background could easily have the effect of cutting off all further discourse with an emotionally loaded epithet.

That a belief in the immanence of the divine may also have reactionary social implications seems to elude not only Starhawk but nearly all ecofeminist writers on the subject. Consider the following sequence of ideas: We accept that the divine is immanent in nature. Human social orders, like human beings themselves, are also part of the natural world. If nonhuman nature is sacred, so too is the human *social* order. If a deity is "immanent" in the cosmos, that deity is "immanent" in society, which must also be seen as part of the cosmos. Thus, the "immanent" divine imparts its divinity to the human social order, just as it does to nonhuman nature. And if the social order is sacred, we cannot change it.

That this sequence of ideas is *more* than hypothetical can be seen in history itself, particularly in ancient Near Eastern and Egyptian cultures. Here human society was indeed seen as embedded in nature as a whole. It was literally regarded as part of the cosmos. "The ancients," writes Henri Frankfort, one of the most distinguished archaeologists and historians of the Near East, "experienced human life as part of a widely spreading network of connections which reached beyond the local and national communities into the hidden depths of nature and the powers that rule nature... Whatever was significant was embedded in the life of the cosmos." An early Egyptian cosmology, the Memphite Theology, for example, in a section on the indissoluble place of society in nature, describes the immanence of the god Ptah in all nature: "He [Ptah] is in every body, in every mouth, of all gods, people, beasts, crawling creatures and whatever else lives." There, as Frankfort observes, "*the order of society* as established by Menes [the first pharaoh] is presented as part of the cosmic order." (emphasis added)[5]

Yet, its firm belief in divine immanence and animism aside, Egypt was a highly oppressive pharaonic theocracy, as we have seen, with a firmly entrenched and overbearing hierarchy. The pharaoh stood at the apex of the hierarchy, and in him the divine was immanent. In fact, he was literally seen as a deity. The rule and person of the divine pharaoh ensured a harmonious integration of nature and society, so the Egyptians believed, none of which prevented the state from demanding blind conformity by everyone, as well as corvée labor by the peasantry. "In Egypt," writes Frankfort, "the community...freed itself from fear and uncertainty by considering its ruler a god. It sacrificed all liberty for the sake of a never changing integration of society and nature."[6] A thoroughly fixed and static conception of a divine immanent in nature was used to justify and integrate a thoroughly hierarchical society based on domination.

The Sumerians also regarded the divine as immanent in the cosmos and society alike. *All* phenomena—including not only living creatures and objects but also society—were ruled by divinely sanctioned "natural laws" called *mes*. Such beliefs persisted into later Mesopotamian cultures after Sumer. "The belief that the gods were immanent in nature was not confined to the pristine age of Mesopotamian religion," writes Frankfort, citing the "An-Anum list," a late Mesopotamian cosmology.[7] Yet this belief in the immanence of the divine will in the cosmos did not prevent the Assyrians, Medes, Persians, and others from developing vast hierarchies, even highly despotic empires in Mesopotamia and Asia. The divine was seen as immanent in the office of kingship (if not in the person of the king himself, as Frankfort points out).[8] With this conception of the divine, the Assyrians built the most rationalized, powerful state machine the ancient world had seen. Indeed, Assyria was the prototypical oriental despotism even as it regarded the divine as immanent in nature and in its social order.

Starhawk assures us, however, that the converse is true—that it is only "in the worldview of power-over" —in which the divine is seen as separate from "nature" —that "human beings have no inherent worth; value must be earned or granted." It is "the split between spirit and matter, which locates God and the sacred outside the world of form and earth and flesh" that "allows exploitation and destruction of human beings and the earth's resources."[9] By this logic, one would expect cultures where the divine is seen as immanent to be those that cherish and highly value human beings.

Alas, however compelling Starhawk's speculative fantasies may seem, her conclusions have surprisingly little support in historical fact. Indeed, it was precisely a belief in the divine as immanent in the cosmos that served to *justify* the oppression of humans in the absolutist terms treasured by ancient priesthoods—just as ideas of a transcendental divine later served to justify monarchies by the "divine right of kings" in the early modern period. But Sumerian and other Mesopotamian cosmologies, their notions of immanence notwithstanding, regarded human beings as worthless, as mere slaves to the gods. In these cosmologies, people had been created solely for the purpose of serving the deities and the divinely immanent social order. Humans, in Mesopotamian cosmology, were degraded from the outset, almost genetically it would seem, according to the terms of their very creation.

Under the aegis of this belief system, Mesopotamian culture was thoroughly ossified, and, under a sacralized absolute despotism, there was nothing human beings could do to change their lot. They had fixed, preordained stations in a static universe that, owing to their complete insignificance, could not be questioned. We can say with reasonable certainty that such resignation and fatalism must have made life miserable for most of the population. In a surviving Mesopotamian text, the "Dialogue of Pessimism" of the first millennium B.C.E., the possiblity of the "good life" is wholly negated. Nothing is seen as good or worthwhile, and all striving is fatalistically seen as vain and futile.

By contrast, in the ancient Near Eastern world, there was a striking exception to the general belief in an immanent divine in nature and society—that of the Hebrews. Indeed, by separating the divine from nature, in a creator god who existed outside his creation—in short, a transcendental deity—the Hebrews were free to view the social order as neither static nor sacred. We may grant that Hebrew culture was patriarchal in its own right and clung to beliefs in a supernature. In this respect, the Hebrew religion, like all religions, was more revelational than rational. But what is truly extraordinary, in contrast to the immanent beliefs of their despotic neighbors, is that by separating Yahweh from nature, the Hebrews also separated the divine from the human social order and thereby *desacralized* society itself. The social order, in effect, became a secular, human, and mutable phenomenon. The ancient Hebrews thus took the first step—a revolutionary step in its day—of making society subject to change, improvement, and human agency. Indeed, it was when the divine came to be seen as *outside* of nature—that is, as transcendental—that the social order could be regarded as malleable. Society, freed of a cosmic "eternal" and static divine, thereby became historical, transitory, and changeable by ordinary people.

The Hebrew religion thus instilled hope, a belief in the possibility of a just society, a utopian sensibility. This hope brought vast expectations that flared into widespread political revolts against authority during the first millennium B.C.E. and afterward, in marked contrast to the fatalism and stagnation that existed in Mesopotamian and Egyptian cultures. By secularizing the world, Hebrew thought laid the earliest basis for social change and even social revolution in Western culture. As historian William McNeill observes, "On the strength of their outward holiness and sustained by inner conviction, they even dared to attack the monarchy and the unrighteousness of the wealthy and powerful." The prophets Amos, Hosea, and the first Isaiah vigorously denounced social abuses, sharply attacked the Hebrew and other kings precisely because, being secular, they were subject to criticism, and served "as specially privileged representatives and spokesmen of the humbler classes in the growingly stratified society of the day."[10]

Thus, the abolition of the immanence of the divine was in fact a first step in the secularization of society. Like it or not, it is nonsense for Starhawk to assert that "spirituality promotes passivity when the domain of spirit is defined as outside the world." The Hebrews were the progenitors of an intensely revolutionary tradition—a step that could not have been taken if they had conceived the divine as immanent in the social order.

Let me make it clear that I am not making a defense of transcendental versus immanent religion per se. To the contrary, although both views have their place in the development of Western consciousness and society, both are inadequate bases for ecological philosophy and activism today. The animism of early nature religions and philosophies is understandable in a time when Western culture still had to disengage itself from a worldview based on a very naive naturalism. The immanence of the divine is also understandable in its historical context. Just so, Hebrew and Christian transcendentalism must be seen within the context of Western culture's developing religious history and its gradual transformation into a secular society. That the Hebrews tried to secularize their society by a transcendental outlook is understandable in an age when religion still encompassed everyone's outlook.

But the immanent goddess that the ecofeminist-theists affirm is regressive not simply because it is a return to theism per se, and not simply because conceptions of the divine as immanent have long reinforced established social orders—albeit Starhawk's claims to the contrary—but also because ecofeminist theism is *cyclical*—this cyclicity presumably being an aspect of the goddess' femaleness. Not only does the immanence of this deity potentially return us to the era of divinely sanctioned social orders; the cyclicity of this deity potentially traps both human beings and the natural world in a cycle of eternal recurrence. In a purely cyclical conception of human and nonhuman nature, the possibility of development is simply foreclosed, and life-forms generally—and human beings particularly—cannot advance beyond preordained conditions. Cyclical theories of nature notoriously freeze humanity in a nature that undergoes no real development and can achieve no fulfillment. This kind of "naturalism" has long been regarded by serious thinkers as extremely reactionary, leading to a denial of any real choice or even the possiblity of progress and miring humanity in a conception of nature that is not only "eternal" but stagnant.

Although today the "idea of progress" is commonly associated with scientific and technological discoveries that are believed to fuel the ecological crisis, it should be emphasized that an idea of progress also underlies utopian thought. Jewish and Christian doctrine, with their tradition of historicity, were open-ended and allowed for this utopian dimension—despite the religious hierarchies that have long marked them—precisely because of their much-maligned "linearity." Again, I am not asking for a return to Jewish and Christian theology, but for an understanding of their emancipatory dimensions in their *historical contexts.* The present era, with its ecological crisis, provides an historical context in which a cyclical, immanent deity can only be regressive. Although the seasons pass in the earthly biosphere, we know today that nature in a broader sense is developmental, not simply cyclical. Our era has seen evolutionary theories of nature emerge in a number of different forms over the past century and a half. We know that human society emerged out of nonhuman nature even as it remains embedded in it. Natural evolution is the indispensable ground from which social evolution emerges, as social ecology shows, and in social ecology's developmental approach, society can be potentially changed to become ecological, even as humans understand their grounding in nonhuman nature. But in the cosmos of the cyclical goddess, human striving is necessarily in vain since everything recurs, and efforts to change the course of events dissolve back into the sameness of eternal recurrence.

The Ethics of "Aliveness"

In reaction to what they see as the prevailing mechanistic worldview that brought about the "death of nature," other ecofeminists propose as an alternative various views of the "aliveness" of the earth or of nonhuman nature. If the mechanistic worldview reduced both human beings and nonhuman nature to instrumentalized resources and allowed the biosphere to be ravaged, the "aliveness" of nature, ecofeminists propose, will teach us to respect nonhuman nature and humans' "interconnectedness" with it. Thus, hylozoism becomes a new ecofeminist cosmology that is seen as having far-reaching ethical implications for human behavior in relation to the nonhuman world.

And to be sure, for much longer than most people realize, Western culture saw the cosmos as a living organism, its various parts interconnected. Some of the ancient Greeks, for example, saw it as "not only a vast animal with a 'soul' of its own, but a rational animal with a 'mind' of its own," as R. G. Collingwood has written.[11] With reference to the Greeks, Collingwood's statement must be taken provisionally—Aristotle, Democritus, Epicurus, and others were important exceptions. But particularly Plato and the more mystical Greek philosophers live up to Collingwood's judgment. Indeed, Plato's cosmology posited a female "world-soul" (despite his misogyny).

Environmental factors prevented Greek hylozoism from becoming a justification for repression in the ancient *polei.* Where imperial and temple cities of the Near East emerged on vast expanses of flat land and in river valleys that made centralization very easy, the Greek *polei* developed in a highly wrinkled mountainous terrain that made for humanly scaled and decentralized communities. Moreover, the Greek *polei* did not develop a priestly caste that was comparable in any way to the huge clerical corporate entities that formed the early basis for Mesopotamian and Egyptian society. The history of Greek thought saw a dramatic transition from mythopoesis to speculative rationalism. Thus, the hylozoistic view of nature of the Greeks played a subordinate role to their more secular political thought and values. Greek nature philosophy, in fact, was more often than not an extension of the Greek *polis* into the cosmos, and traditional religious festivals were increasingly permeated by civic characteristics.

In imperial Rome, hylozoism was to come very much into vogue, particularly among the neo-Platonist philosophers. Plotinus inherited Plato's concept of a female "world-soul"—literally the soul of the world as female, animate, intelligent, and good—and it became an important part of this philosopher's cosmology. Although much Christian doctrine distinguished between the living and the nonliving, Christian culture coexisted with a rather hylozoistic view of nonhuman nature that it had inherited from Plotinus by way of Augustine (who tended to rely heavily on Neoplatonism for answers to questions not addressed in Scripture). Hylozoistic cosmology persisted until the Renaissance and beyond, even into the thinking of some of the founders of modern science.

In Western culture, as Collingwood points out, the view that the universe is alive was based on an analogy—an analogy between the universe and an organism. According to this traditional way of viewing the cosmos, the universe-organism was the "macrocosm," and the human being-organism to which it was analogous was the "microcosm." As Hans Jonas observes of such macrocosms,

> As the generative life-begetting powers of nature bespeak the presence of soul, and the eternal regularity and harmony of the celestial motions the action of an ordering mind, the world must be considered as one animated and intelligent whole, and even as wise.[12]

The ancient Roman Stoics, who inherited this macrocosm-microcosm theory from certain Greek schools, accordingly believed that "nature" was alive. As Cicero wrote,

> What can be more foolish than to deny that that Nature which comprehends all things is the most excellent, or, if this is granted, to deny that it is *firstly animate,* secondly rational and reflective, and thirdly wise? How else could it be the most excellent? (emphasis added)[13]

For Stoics like Cicero, the living cosmos, as good, contained an ethical imperative for human beings to behave in accordance with it, to "adequate" themselves to it, in Jonas's word. Indeed, in imperial Rome, it was common for people to be *less* concerned with their place in society than they were with their cosmological place in nature. The Stoic injunction to "live consistently with nature" was meant to have ethical force because the universe was seen as the highest expression of morality. The Stoics, it appeared, lived by the very precepts ecofeminists advocate: a living cosmos as such was ethical, and human beings obliged to live in accordance with it.

But the "living" cosmos of the Stoics did not produce the effects that ecofeminists claim result from hylozoism, any more than was the case with divine immanence. Indeed, the Stoics had little expectation that humans could change society at all. Stoicism is above all a philosopy of resignation, fatalism, and quiescence. In "adequating" themselves to the cosmos, they were guided by the principle of apathy, not activity, except in the inner recesses of their private lives, as the writings of Epictetus so clearly demonstrate. The individual in declining Roman society could no more make a difference in the cosmos—or in society, for that matter—than could ordinary Mesopotamians and Egyptians millennia earlier.

I am certain that neither Starhawk nor ecofeminist theologian Carol P. Christ willingly supports tyranny of any kind, but the values of "aliveness" and "immanence" that these ecofeminist-the-ists offer have implications that are not intrinsically liberatory as ethical prescriptions. Indeed, the Stoic Seneca fatalistically com-mitted suicide at the orders of Nero. Some of Carol P. Christ's ruminations hint at just the kind of passive attitude one would have expected of an ancient Roman Stoic. "With regard to life and death there is no ultimate justice, nor ultimate injustice," she writes, "for there is no promise that life will be other than it is." Her fatalistic admonitions echo the terrible sense of individual powerlessness of Stoic cosmology and hardly reinforce an outlook that calls for social activism. "Knowledge that we are but a small part of life and death and transformation is the essential religious insight," Christ tells us. "We are no more valuable to the life of the universe than a field flowering in the color purple." The Roman emperors Augustus and Nero could have expected no greater passivity of their subjects.[14]

Medieval natural philosophy and science did much to elabo-rate the macrocosm-microcosm theory—indeed, so much so that the correspondence between the human being as a microcosm and the vast reaches of the universe as an organismic macrocosm became, as Theodore Spencer puts it, "a medieval platitude."[15] If a mere belief that nature is alive has emancipatory consequences, this was certainly not the case in the late Middle Ages, when the hierarchicalism and power of the Church and the nobles reached their zenith. The macrocosm-microcosm theory, in fact, came to be intertwined with the Great Chain of Being and both in tandem with each other helped provide a far-reaching justification for the existence of hierarchy in society as a whole. Analogies were made, for example, between God as the lord of creation and humans as lords of the earth; the human, located midway between God and the inorganic on the Great Chain, could only aspire to know God and possibly become like his subordinate angels.

Surprisingly, Carolyn Merchant regards the Great Chain of Being itself as an organismic concept, as a "living chain of being."[16] Whether one agrees that the Great Chain of Being can justifiably be considered organismic, it certainly was a top-down approach and was much intertwined with the macrocosm-microcosm theory. Although Merchant rightly observes that Aquinas, basing his cosmology on the Great Chain of Being—and by implication the macrocosm-microcosm theory—elaborated "an integrated system of nature and society," the fact is that it was hierarchical (as Merchant acknowledges), contrary to what we would suppose from Starhawk's notion of an organismic theory of the cosmos. Again, Aquinas must also be seen in his day and time, when hierarchical cosmologies reflected a hierarchic feudal society.

Just as the immanent divine in the Near East served to reinforce social notions of hierarchy, so the microcosm-macrocosm theory and the Great Chain of Being served to reinforce hierarchy in the Middle Ages up to Elizabethan England. Ironically, there is a basic contradiction between Merchant's work—which shows that Western cosmology was often organismic before the early modern period—and that of ecofeminists like Starhawk who argue that a concept of "nature" as "alive" has *innately* antihierarchical consequences. Again, from all we have seen, the very reverse can be true. We must always remind ourselves that worldviews cannot be reduced to vague abstractions that are free from any historical context and the forms of social order they either reinforce or challenge.

Insofar as Merchant's scholarly book *The Death of Nature* attempts to show the transition from an organismic to a mechanistic worldview, it is highly informative. But the extent to which organismic worldviews that were specifically female preceded the Scientific Revolution, as a casual reading of Merchant might suggest, is questionable. Starting with the first sentence of her book, "Women and nature have an age-old association," the casual reader may come away from this loose statement with the impression that *nature as a whole* was regarded as both female and living in Western cosmology up until the Scientific Revolution. Merchant artfully intersperses literary images of the earth as female, Alan de Lille's Goddess Natura (a medieval literary allegory) and other allegorical figures, and cosmologies of Plato's world-soul—all of which are indeed female—with organismic concepts of nature that were not gendered at all.

Thus, the reader should be alert to the subtleties of Merchant's presentation. To be sure, the earth per se was long seen as female, whether in the sense of a deity or as a poetic metaphor. That Merchant can demonstrate this is not surprising. And to be sure, organismic conceptions of nature were longstanding in Western culture—this too is no surprise, as R. G. Collingwood and Hans Jonas, among others, wrote decades ago. But perceptions of Merchant's book that suggest that a *living, female, conception of nature preceded the Scientific Revolution* are highly problematic indeed.

For one thing, the concepts "nature" and "earth" cannot be used interchangeably. Nonhuman nature—let alone "nature" in the sense of cosmology—is more than "Mother Earth." The "female-ness" of "Mother Earth" cannot be extended to the universe as a whole, or to nature conceived as the macrocosm. From a cosmolog-ical viewpoint, macrocosmic nature includes not only the earth but also the sun, stars, and other celestial bodies, as well as principles of organization and development that are not exclusively premised on organismic principles.

Second, to claim that a macrocosmic conception of nature as both living and female prevailed before the early modern period is not supported even in Merchant's own book, let alone in the history of ideas itself. For example, despite Plato's female world-soul and its incorporation into Neoplatonism, and despite Neoplatonism's influence on Augustine, Christianity did not preserve the female-ness of an organismic macrocosm. If anything, the prevailing organismic conceptions of nature before the Scientific Revolution—the correspondence theories—were genderless or male. If the *microcosm*—the individual human being—was gendered, the *macrocosm*—the universe as a whole—was at best a composite of both genders.

Elizabethan England (which was occupied with constructing one of Europe's earliest nation-states) commonly saw the various patterns, designs, and functions of the human body—not strictly the female body—as replicated in the realms of the cosmos and extended to the universe as a whole. There were exact analogies for humans' organic and bodily functions, "correspondences" between the human body and the body of the world, as well as between the human soul and the soul of the universe. If God created the universe from four elements—earth, air, fire and water—the human "microcosm" was composed from the same. For every organ, every bone, every function of the several parts of the human body, there were correspondences. (One is reminded of Spretnak's flighty geography of the female body.) It is little wonder that Elizabethan literature reached the spectacularly rich metaphorical heights it did (although by no means free of ghosts, superstitions, and childish fables).

For the Elizabethan Walter Raleigh, whose *History of the World* reflects the thought of his time, human flesh corresponded to the earth; human bones to rocks; blood to brooks and rivers; and breath to air. Human body heat corresponded to the earth's internal heat. Human hair corresponded to grass; reproductive organs corresponded to the generative powers of "nature." Human eyes corresponded to the light of the sun and moon. The human head corresponded to God and the intelligible universe itself, not only in its shape but by virtue of being the seat of reason. "Both the world and the universe were repeated in the structure of man's body," writes Theodore Spencer. "In his 'round head,' a copy of the sphere of the universe, man might find the whole cosmic system written in small with mystical meaning." Thoughts corresponded to the motions of the angels, and for Raleigh,

> Our pure understanding (formally called Mens,
> and that which always looketh upwards)
> [corresponded] to those intellectual Natures,
> which are always present with God: and...Our
> immortal Souls (while they are righteous) are by
> God himself beautified with the Title of his own
> Image and Similitude.[17]

The notion that the world macrocosm was specifically female, then, can hardly be justified on the basis of these and many other similar remarks. In Elizabethan England, this was the concept that the Scientific Revolution eliminated, and however organismic, its gender is ambiguous and cannot be interpreted as strictly female.

The Decay of Nature

Obviously, no organism lives forever. And the world, conceived as alive, could not be eternal either, particularly for the many who believed in an organismic worldview based on naive correspondences. After the end of Elizabeth's reign, the early 17th century in England was "a time when pessimism about man's situation had reached a kind of climax," writes Spencer.[18] Just as human beings are born, grow, and die, so, it was thought, does the world. The idea that the world had been born and had grown—and now was subject to decay—says historian of ideas Richard Jones, "proved useful in affording [people] a convincing explanation of the many evils which met their eyes."[19]

Decay, or senescence, applied not only to the earth but to the universe and everything in it: to celestial bodies, the air, water, plants, animals, minerals, and human beings. The "birth" and "youth" of the earth or universe—like the "birth" and "youth" of humanity—was seen as belonging to the distant past. And the era of the 17th century—what was seen as the decaying state of the world organism—compared poorly indeed with the ancient past, it was widely believed. Even Adam, despite his sin, for example, had lived to be 999 years old, and the classical Greeks seemed like giants compared with the people of early 17th-century society. The decay of nature seemed to explain the many social problems of the day, like poverty and the hardness of life. Indeed, the view that the macrocosm had definitely reached the stage of old age was quite widespread in England and elsewhere at this time.

An important symptom of this decay was the appearance of "new stars" in the heavens. It had been an integral part of the old cosmology that the heavens were immutable. Corresponding to the angels, and "intellectual natures" to which human reason could aspire, the motions of the stars had been seen as eternal in the supralunar realm. Only in the sublunar realm—the realm below the moon, which included the earth and all things on it—had change and decay previously been thought possible. "Change and decay had always been limited to matter lying beneath the orb of the moon. The heavens, the handiwork of God, were eternal and immutable," as historian of science Herbert Butterfield writes.[20]

But the appearance in 1572 of a "new star" in Cassiopeia and in 1604 in Serpentarius gave the lie to this doctrine. Aristotle had said there could be no new stars, no new appearances of any kind in the eternal heavens, and Christians had accepted only one "new star" : the star of Bethlehem, which appeared at the time of the birth of Christ. The presence of "new stars," however, did much to convince people that nature was in a state of decay and that the universe was coming to an end.

A fundamental quarrel took place between those who believed in the decay of nature (called the "ancients," because they believed people in the ancient world were superior to their 17th-century contemporaries) and those who believed that nature was constant (the "moderns," who thought humanity could improve). For the "ancients," decaying humanity could not hope to improve its condition. "Probably no single factor was so responsible for the feeling of modern inferiority as the belief that all nature was decaying in its old age," writes Richard Jones.[21] In their worship of antiquity, "Men seemed to be blind to any possible virtues in their own time." But for the "moderns," new knowledge was not only possible but necessary. The "moderns" believed that it was precisely the constancy of nature's laws that made it possible for humans to have a sense of optimism about the future. Indeed, the "modern" George Hakewill in 1627 was obliged to argue against the organismic-correspondence analogy to explain the stars and the heavens, the earth, and the nature of human accomplishment throughout history. Hakewill argued, in Jones' paraphrase, that "decay is not the order of the day; men have accomplished much, and they have an *active* role to play in their own improvement and in that of the earth." (emphasis added)[22] If there was to be any forward-looking attitude, any progress in improving the miserable lot of human beings, the moderns argued, it was necessary to believe in the *constancy* of nature and in the regular operation of its laws, not in its decay.

To the contrary of what Starhawk proposes it was not "living with the knowledge that the cosmos is alive" that caused people "to do something." Rather, the very opposite was true. Within the context of the 17th century, the notion that "nature" operated according to constant laws that humans could understand gave them hope of improving their miserable lot. It was this view, given the historical time when it was advanced and the limitations that burden it, that caused people to advocate "doing something" about the misery around them. Admittedly, the "moderns'" optimism and their reliance on nature's constancy contributed greatly to the rise of modern science, and to the mechanistic worldview that de-stroyed the organismic cosmology. But in doing so, it also helped destroy a cosmology that validated a hierarchical social order and whose decay filled people with despair and fueled the intolerances of the era, including the persecution of women as witches. Despite the serious limitations of the mechanistic worldview, we cannot ignore the fact that *in its day* it gave humanity a source of hope and optimism, replacing a naive decaying-organism cosmology that was infusing them with a deep sense of resignation.

The Ethics of Vitalism

Although Carolyn Merchant laments the "the death of nature as a living being"—the end of the organic worldview with "a view of nature [as] a kindly and caring motherly provider"[23]—she does not explicitly advocate the literal restoration of the images, their archaic values, or the organismic cosmologies so prevalent in the pre-capitalist past. Although "the image of nature as a nurturing mother contain[ed] ethical implications" in its day and its framework was "for many centuries sufficiently integrative to override commercial development and technological innovation," Merchant writes, social factors changed in the modern era with the commercial revolution, and "the values associated with the organic view of nature were no longer applicable."[24] Presumably, her *Death of Nature* intends merely "to examine the values associated with the images of women and nature as they relate to the formation of our modern world and their implications for our lives today."[25]

But these statements become ambiguous when Merchant leads us to believe that certain "vitalistic" views of nature have an inherently liberatory ethical force. She attributes some of the same "normative" characteristics that other ecofeminists attribute to hylozoism and divine immanence to the kind of "vitalism" with which she seems to sympathize.

> Vitalism in its monistic form was *inherently antiexploitative.* Its emphasis on the life of all things as gradations of soul, its lack of a separate distinction between matter and spirit, its principle of an immanent activity permeating nature, and its reverence for the nurturing power of the earth endowed it with an ethic of the inherent worth of everything alive. Contained within the conceptual structure of vitalism was a *normative* constraint. (emphasis added)[26]

The vitalist philosophy with which Merchant is sympathetic is not that of the well-known vitalists of the 19th and 20th centuries, like Bergson and Driesch. Rather, her sympathies are with a circle of late-17th-century thinkers that included Gottfried Wilhelm von Leibniz.[27] Leibniz's "dynamic vitalism," for Merchant, was in direct opposition to the "death of nature." In this vitalistic component of his later thought we find an organic orientation which...can be construed as antiexploitative; normative constraints are contained within the framework itself and imposed by it. His principle of self-contained internal development central to the organic world view sharply contrasted with the mechanistic theory that change is reactive—the product of external influences on a passive entity.[28]

As Merchant notes, Leibniz proposed in his cosmology that life and perception permeate all things; he regarded all of reality—inorganic and organic—as made up of an infinite number of the living points he called monads. To be sure, there are many interesting aspects to Leibniz's philosophy, including his notion that these living monads are characterized by a self-active unfolding, and a *conatus,* or life-urge; they exist in a mentalistic progression from vegetative and sensitive to rational.

Merchant presents these monads as operating according to what could be construed as a beguiling ecofeminist model of consensus, self-organization, and harmony.

The actions of the Leibnizian monads exist in a continual state of mutual harmony...the overall result is a consensus of individual actions producing that which is best for the whole and the maximization of perfection in the world. Each monad mirrors the universe in its own way, its life unfolding simultaneously with the lives of all other monads in a pre-established harmony.[29]

Here we come to some real problems. Leibniz, to be sure, did see monads as acting harmoniously, and their lives did "unfold simultaneously with the lives of all other monads." But the reader should be warned that by "consensus," Leibniz did not mean that these monads interact with each other intersubjectively, much less

consciously organize themselves into a harmonious whole. For
Leibniz, the subjectivity of the monads was one of complete isolation from one another; indeed, their isolation does not allow for
any communication among them. As one historian of philosophy
has put it, "the fact that each Monad is thus held incommunicado
and is unable to interact or directly communicate wih its fellows
is freely admitted by Leibniz....Each one is hermetically sealed up
within itself."[30] The changes that monads undergo result from their
pre-formed natures. (This is, in fact, the picture of the Leibnizian
monad as a self-enclosed bourgeois ego.)

The "pre-established harmony" to which Merchant refers, the
harmony in which the monads' lives unfold, is pre-established
indeed—but *by God, not by the monads themselves.* Theirs is not
a self-organized order, but an order imposed from without. Merchant tries to get around this problem by arguing that the monads
unfold according to an "internal law from which their actions and
passions follow," but this is begging the question[31]—it remains
God's order, however indirect, for Leibniz wrote that "a prevenient
divine contrivance...from the beginning has formed each of these
substances in a way so perfect, and regulated with so much accu-
racy, that merely by following laws of its own...it nevertheless
agrees with the other, just as if...God in addition to his general
cooperation constantly put his hand thereto."[32]

Nor does this "vitalism" have the "inherently anti-exploitative" characteristics Merchant assigns to it. Since this "pre-established harmony" (however indirectly) derives from God, and God
is good, Leibniz argued, the reality that the monads form must be
"the best of all possible worlds." Merchant attempts to cast this in
a progressive light by attributing it to the Enlightenment's "optimism over the progress of human civilization and the internal
development of the universe as a whole."[33] But even seen in this
historical context, Merchant is stretching Leibniz's "progressiv-
ism" rather thin. For Leibniz's tendencies were much more acqui-
escent to the status quo than Merchant would lead us to believe.
He thought that "we must be really satisfied with all that comes to
us according to [God's] will," and he was hardly "anti-exploitative"
when he wrote disapprovingly of "those who are not satisfied with

what God does," for they "seem to me [Leibniz] like dissatisfied subjects whose attitude is not very different from that of rebels."[34] Philosopher John Herman Randall, Jr., notes that although Leibniz's belief that we are living in "the best of all possible worlds" is sometimes called an optimistic belief, it "strikes many as being the height of pessimism: if it is, God help the human race!"[35] Like the organismic worldviews in the pre-capitalist world—based on correspondences—that we have discussed, Leibniz's "vitalism" also lacks the "normative constraints" that Merchant attributes to it. If anything, it is marked by a depressing acquiescence to the status quo—a view that Voltaire hilariously mocked in his classic short story *Candide*.

Conclusion

Both Starhawk's hylozoism and Merchant's Leibnizian "vitalist" sympathies fall into the trap of reacting so fervently against the "deadness" of Cartesian mechanism that they reduce reality to the other extreme—namely, the "aliveness" of everything. Just as the mechanistic worldview ignored the organic aspects of the world of nature, these neo-hylozoisms ignore its mechanical aspects. Both mechanism and hylozoism are one-sided fallacies, and as a result of either, our thinking dissolves into a simplistic reductionism in which the cosmos is either dead or alive, completely mechanical or completely organismic, completely atomized or completely interconnected to the point of a oneness in which distinctions among the various phenomena that constitute the world are difficult to make. They lack a developmental perspective and deprive us of any sense of the emergence, differentiation, and cumulative elaboration of different potentialities in both realms.

We need more than loose and simplistic metaphors like "aliveness" and "divine immanence" —and more than neo-"vitalistic" principles—to adequately formulate an ecological philosophy for our own time. If we are going to have an ethics grounded in nature, it has to be based on our best understanding of the natural world, particularly of natural evolution, and of the social world, not on an atavistic revival of archaic concepts of nature from the past. People in earlier times, like Elizabethan England, believed that the world was an organism by correspondence because that was the best knowledge they had of nature—and they believed they could legitimately understand nature through macrocosm-micro-cosm analogies. The mere fact that their ideas were organic or "alive" and "divinely immanent" did not make them more correct than mechanistic views. The fallacy of ecofeminists who adhere to Starhawk's free-wheeling method of substituting vague metaphors for ideas is that they have produced childish correspondence theories of their own.

That broad divisions can be made between an organismic cosmology and a mechanistic one is certainly valid, provided that we do not assume that every one of these outlooks necessarily plays the same role at all times in history. It is obvious, for example, that the transcendentalism of the Hebrews opened an enormous breach in the all-encompassing immanent divine of the Near East that fostered apathy and resignation, while organismic-correspondence theories, which played an oppressive role in earlier centuries, were challenged by mechanistic ones that played a liberating role in their own time. Merely to say that the world is "alive" degenerates into a metaphor when we know in fact that distinctions must be drawn between what is living and what is nonliving in the world today as well as how they are interrelated. An organismic theory that is not developed out of a comprehensive understanding of the history of ideas, of society, and of nature can be as paralyzing as mechanistic theories that do little more than reduce living things and the world to clockwork.

Ironically, the most significant challenge to mechanism as a worldview—the philosophy and science of evolution, as they began with Darwin in the nineteenth century—is virtually ignored in Merchant's book, as in ecofeminist writings generally. Dialecti-cal and developmental thinking—drawing on evolutionary think-ing as in a dialectical naturalist approach—provides a much-needed understanding of the clearly *graded* developments in nature and society from the inorganic to the organic, and from the organic to the social. As we shall see, such an approach is necessary if we are to educe these gradations and avoid the reductionist extremes at either end of the philosophical spectrum.

To be sure, there is a continuity between nonhuman and human nature, and there are certain basic concepts of ecology—such as unity in diversity, spontaneity, and nonhierarchical relationships—that can apply both to the organic world and to an ethics for an ecological society. But there are also certain human attributes that exist only in nascent form in the nonhuman world that are essential to human freedom. As such, human freedom requires, for example, a commitment to democratic practice, which is not contained in ecofeminist normative prescriptions of the "immanent divine" or the "alive." Lacking such an approach, ecofeminist ethics remains mired in simplistic, metaphoric, and naive one-to-one correspondences between nonhuman nature and human society. To construct an ecological ethics around such correspondences ignores the distinctions between them. Concepts of hylozoism, cyclicity, and divine immanence have served to validate hierarchy just as easily as have transcendental religions and mechanistic cosmologies. Taken by themselves, they are not "inherently" liberatory for human beings. Nor need they follow an emancipatory logic of their own, apart from the historical conditions in which they exist. History shows that these ideas can be extremely reactionary and foster quietism rather than activism.

Many ecofeminists may find it comforting to accept disparate notions of a divinely immanent or living world that meant one thing in the Neolithic, another in the ancient Near East, and still another in the medieval and Elizabethan worlds. But the simple fact is that these worldviews were not true in the light of what we know today and cannot be revived in a time like our own that has a very rich knowledge of the natural world. That a worldview is organismic does not automatically give it an authority that allows us to ignore the complexities and challenges that are required of us in developing an emancipatory and ecological ethics today. In sum, we must accept or reject ideas and cosmologies not simply on the basis of any ethical force that they are *presumed* to have but on the basis of whether they correctly explain the world around us. What is wrong with hylozoism, vitalism, and divine immanence, particularly when any of them are associated with women, is that they are false in terms of what we now know. Ultimately, the universe, the solar system, and the earth are not living organisms, however much there may be life in the cosmos. And no use of the word "inherent" can deny this simple natural truth.

Chapter 4

Mythopoesis and the Irrational

Scientific reason, for some ecofeminists, is a kind of mentation that violates the spirit of nature's wholeness and aliveness. It "divides" that which is not divisible, they say. It conceptually separates aspects of reality that are actually inseparable. It analyzes and fragments, seeking out and emphasizing the differences between things, rather than the commonalities they share. It examines parts instead of wholes. But nature, say such ecofeminists, does not reflect these separations. Reality, for Susan Griffin, knows no boundaries, only wholeness, for "between my arm and the air, between the movements of a flame and what we call the solid mass of wood, there is no boundary." This state of boundarylessness is not only physical but emotive: "We are connected not only by the fact of our dependency on this biosphere and our participation in one field of matter and energy...but also by what we know and what we feel."

The wholeness and interconnectedness of nature makes certain unifying modes of subjectivity very appealing to many ecofeminists, forms of subjectivity that are presumably more suitable to understanding wholes. One such unifying mode is an epistemology that is experiential and that focuses on the concrete rather than on the general or the universal, to intuit a thing's being. Griffin's approach to knowledge seeks "a union with what we perceive" in experience. Giving attention to sensual rather than measurable qualities, for Griffin, is "evidence of a profound, sensual, and emotional connection we have with all that is part of this earth...The joy color gives us is perhaps part of the balance of the universe."[1]

Doubtless one of the great projects of human thought has been the attempt to *transcend* the dualities that exist in objective reality and in thinking, indeed long before ecofeminists got hold of this philosophical enterprise. But great dialectical thinkers like Aristotle and Hegel recognized that to understand a fully developed whole, one must recognize that it emerged from a process of ever-greater differentiation. Indeed, they understood that wholes develop from "dualities," a term that should be distinguished from "dualism" as a philosophical school of thought. The divisions between subject and object, good and evil, feeling and intellect, as Hegel showed, are indispensable phases (or "moments") in the process of differentiation and the formation of more *complete,* richly articulated, and fully developed wholes. Wholes or unities emerge out of and contain those very divisions—that are often called "dualisms" by less sophisticated writers—and that are essential in any development.

I will take up the nature of dialectical thinking in a later chapter, but suffice it to say here that it is premised on contradiction that terminates through a developmental process in wholeness. But it is fallacious to regard everything, as do such unifying modes of consciousness as Griffin's, as *so* whole and "interconnected" that one no longer recognizes the very "dualities" and conflicts that enter into a development and culminate in a richly articulated whole. To declare that "between my arm and the air, between the movements of a flame and what we call the solid mass of wood, there is no boundary" is to unthinkingly dissolve all particularities and real boundaries between things that must ultimately be negated, assimilated, and transcended.

For theistic ecofeminists, Griffin's unifying intuitions become intuitions of "oneness" and "divine immanence," in the realm of a supernature that can only be discovered through mystical experiences. Charlene Spretnak regards the "true nature of being" as a "oneness" that can be apprehended by "the subtle, suprarational reaches of mind.

> All is One, all forms of existence are comprised
> of one continuous dance of matter/energy arising
> and falling away, arising and falling away. Only
> the illusions of separation divide us. The
> experience of union with the One has been called
> cosmic consciousness, God consciousness,
> knowing the One Mind, etc.[2]

Spretnak's goddess, who "symbolizes the way things really are: All
forms of being are One," is designed to help congregants of both
sexes get in touch with this coveted "oneness." Religious rituals
and chants are very useful, needless to say, apparently in cultivating those "suprarational reaches of mind." Such "suprarationality"
culminates in faith in a supernatural being, obliterating not only
boundaries between human bodies and their environment but
between nature and supernature.

By promising that "ecstasy is at the heart of Witchcraft,"
Starhawk, too, seeks to help women cultivate "levels of consciousness beyond the rational." After all, "the mysteries of the absolute
can never be explained—only felt or intuited."[3] Starhawk seeks to
cultivate these "levels of consciousness beyond the rational" by
using magic, which she feels is "the art of liberation." She asks us
to cultivate our "openness to mystery" by chanting, breathing
together, and the like. Forms of mentation like criticism or self-crit-
icism are harshly discouraged. "We can say something like, 'All
you voices…telling us we're bad or wrong or stupid or crazy—leave
right now!'" she declaims peremptorily. Once this is accomplished,
to "increase the power of this banishing, accompany the word with
shouts, yells, foot-stomping," and the like.[4]

Ecofeminist-theists like Riane Eisler advance still another
unifying mode of consciousness. Inasmuch as our most fundamental processes of mentation are mythopoeic, Eisler seeks to disseminate new myths like those of the Neolithic. "It can be a fatal error
to underestimate the power of myth," she argues.

> The human psyche seems to have a built-in need
> for a system of stories and symbols that 'reveal'

> to us the order of the universe and tell us what
> our place within it is....The problem is...what
> kinds of symbols and myths are to fill and guide
> our minds.

Indeed myth, according to Eisler, can help us find "an opening into the archetypal world" to the ecologically harmonious goddess-worldview. "Through the reaffirmation and celebration of the transformative mysteries... new myths will reawaken in us that lost sense of gratitude and the celebration of life so evident in the artistic remnants of the Neolithic and Minoan Crete."[5]

The striking similarity in language, metaphors, and the yearning literary style that characterizes ecofeminist writings is by no means accidental. As a body of ideas, ecofeminism itself is based on a metaphorical mode of consciousness that stretches words to almost meaningless lengths to bury the massive contradictions between psycho-biologism and social construction, between theism and secularism. Metaphor, in this case, serves the function of unifying disparate tendencies into a mystical mood-language that is more shadowy than clear, presumably constituting an ineffable "unity" in its diversity. Metaphors are normally part of the realm of art and poetry, to be sure, but one of the functions of a political movement, let alone a radical one, is to explain the world, not to obscure it; to provide an analysis of the causes of various developments in society, not to dissolve causes into an obscurantist medley of verbiage. Most 19th- and 20th-century radical social and political movements have at least tried to analyze and explain actual events and social relations, however much they differed with each other. Marxists, dubious as their explanation of how social change is to come about seems today, were very specific about detailing and analyzing the actual exploitation of workers; they used metaphors very sparingly. Although some of the roots and organizing of the 1960s civil rights movement was done in churches, the movement was very specific in its analysis of the exclusion of blacks from personhood in the United States. Early radical feminists made similarly analytical examinations of the institutions—marriage, family, church—that were the causes of women's oppression.

Doubtless, even political movements, particularly in our own century, consciously used metaphors and myth for their great evocative, propagandistic, and even theatrical value. The early 20th-century theorist Georges Sorel used a myth—the General Strike—quite consciously to organize a radical workers' movement. In the 1960s, continual analogies were made between students and the proletariat, between students and blacks, and between women and colonized peoples in Third World countries. While these metaphors may have helped convey certain dubious inspirational concepts, eventually they did not serve these movements well. Quite to the contrary. "Student as nigger" and "student as proletarian" metaphors greatly obscured the realities of the social situation of privileged middle-class white students, let alone of highly deprived blacks and workers. Indeed, they actually served to confuse these realities, as destructive conflicts to make these metaphors tangible within the 1960s student movement so amply demonstrated.

Despite this sorry history of camouflaging reality with metaphors in politics, the ecofeminist movement consciously uses the metaphor of "women = nature," a phrase that has been elaborated by many ecofeminists into an epic cosmology. Indeed, Starhawk regards feminism itself as "a magicospiritual movement as well as a political movement."[6] The ecofeminist metaphor, like other political metaphors of the past, may have a great deal of theatrical value, but metaphors and mythopoesis have often been major obstructions in trying to arrive at the truth and reality of the human condition. Perhaps the major irrationalism of ecofeminism is that blatantly contradictory ideas are to be accepted as "diverse" parts of a "whole." Ultimately, the only way to "reconcile" these irreconcilables is to reject reason as such and to unite them under the spell of intuition and mysticism. Nor are these irreconcilables a dialectical "union of opposites"; they are outright contradictions in *any* system of logic, be it dialectical or formal.

By seeking modes of subjectivity that unify these outright contradictions, ecofeminism often fosters blatant irrationality. The groups of congregants that Starhawk creates under the rubric of "magic," for example, have a mind of sorts, but it is not the minds of the congregants as individuals. Rather, the mind of the group resides in one or a few people—in what Starhawk delicately calls its "responsive leadership." After all, "a group, as an entity with its own spirit and identity, needs a brain. It needs some people...who lead in the sense of stepping out in front and going first."[7] Of course, even the most politically naive reader will recognize that these "responsive leaders," who form the "brain" of the group, are an elite with considerable power to manipulate the merely intuiting congregants.

Cultivation of the irrational can produce extremely reactionary results. Consider the following ritual injunction by a prominent ecofeminist writer, Deena Metzger:

> With your eyes closed, imagine yourself as a tree. Allow the human in yourself to dissolve. Feel your roots going down to the core of the earth, the strength of the trunk here on earth and the branches reaching to the sky. Allow yourself to be a tree and let that be sufficient.[8]

Nowhere is it clearer than in Metzger's ritual injunction that intuitions of interconnectedness are attained at the price of eliminating the rational—and indeed, the human itself. For human beings of whatever sex who are interested in creating an ecological society, it is in no way "sufficient" to "allow" oneself to "be a tree." At this nadir of irrationalism, of willful ignorance and passivity, ecology loses the "critical edge" that Murray Bookchin announced it had in his pioneering 1964 article, "Ecology and Revolutionary Thought."[9] Ecofeminist mystics—some of whom are doubtless well intentioned—need to be wary of their claims for a more advanced human understanding in the light of such blatantly primitivistic ritual injunctions that many tribal people would disdain as a caricature of their traditional beliefs.

Mythopoesis

Unifying modes of subjectivity such as mysticism, metaphor, and myth are all "mythopoeic" in that they try to "unify" phenomena and ideas at the *expense* of differentiations. By emphasizing resemblances among things, they cultivate those faculties of human subjectivity that are incapable of distinguishing between symbol and symbolized, between self and other, between dream and reality, between appearance and the authentic world (both natural and social). In ancient mythopoesis, as Henri and H. A. Frankfort note, "whatever is capable of affecting mind, feeling, or will has thereby established its undoubted reality. There is, for instance, no reason why dreams should be considered less real than impressions received while one is awake."[10] By the same token, advocates of mythopoesis today crudely blur distinctions between illusion and the existential world, even between supernature and nature.

Let me emphasize that fantasy, intuitions, metaphor, and poetry are important parts of human subjectivity, without which human life is neither full nor rich. Who would not agree about the importance of a rich fantasy life, a rich intuitive appreciation, of an imagination? Who would not agree about the aesthetic beauties of the natural world? And there are certainly dimensions of nonhuman nature about which science does not know because it only measures, as philosophers and ecologists generally have argued for decades, if not centuries. There are a wealth of qualities, interconnections, feelings, sensitivities, and subjectivities in nature to which we can respond with appreciation and respect.

Nor should all previous cosmologies in Western history be written off as "untrue" and consigned to a dustbin. They played an important role in the development of science and philosophy as we know them today. For centuries, great mystics like John Scotus Erigena preserved dialectical thinking for later generations to elaborate. Science *is* the history of science, as social ecology argues, and early modern scientists were often mystics, whose intuitions sometimes helped them conceptualize what they would later prove scientifically (but at other times obstructed them). Moreover, we may legitimately use metaphors to help us understand things simply by providing images needed to envision them. Metaphor helps us understand how evolution has progressed, for example— we describe it as like a "tree" that has many "branches." But we know that this is, after all, *only* metaphor even while we use it. We know quite clearly that evolution is not literally a "tree."

By contrast, in its own time, hylozoism—the analogy between the earth or nature as a living being—was more than analogy or metaphor; it was literally seen as truth. People had believed in the organismic analogy since ancient times because to the best of their knowledge, they actually thought the cosmos was an organism. In the Elizabethan era, writes Marjorie Hope Nicholson, "the world was not *like* an animal; it *was* animate."[11] In medieval times, analogies were used for healing because to the best of people's knowledge, they thought analogies explained physiological functioning. Quinces, a hairy fruit, were believed to cure baldness— by analogy. Scorpion-grass, which was shaped like the crooked tail of a scorpion, was thought to heal the bites of poisonous insects—by analogy. Eating walnuts was thought to be good for head wounds because the walnut looks like the human head—again, by analogy.[12] But we know today that medical healing does not work in that way, just as we know that the cosmos is not alive. "Cures" for baldness based on quinces—as poetic and lovely as that notion may be—do not cure baldness, because in harsh reality healing does not work by mere analogies. We know that the earth is not literally a living being, just as we know, for that matter, that the earth is not a machine.

As for myths, earlier European peoples used them to explain important questions like the origin of the cosmos and of human beings. To them, myth had greater meaning than we impute to the word today. Generally, these peoples were not consciously disseminating falsehoods, any more than Elizabethan peoples consciously disseminated falsehoods about quinces. They used myths for their explanatory, as well as for their felt ethical importance. When it came to the hard facts of everyday life, it should be noted, tribal peoples also knew how to build effective shelter for protection and how to efficiently kill game and gather plants for food. Their use of instrumental reasoning is more extensive than people who romanticize them often care to believe, and indeed, their unexcelled pragmatic skills often earn the admiration of Western anthropologists to this very day.

Today, we may certainly appreciate certain myths viewed in their proper historical context. Even though we no longer literally believe the contents of stories of Ishtar and Demeter, their myths, to modern eyes, nonetheless bear a strong aesthetic appeal, and their existence can tell us a great deal about the evolution of modern consciousness. We can respect the place of myth in tribal cultures that ground them in authentic traditions. But whether we like it or not, myths, mythopoesis, and magic no longer serve the explanatory functions today that they seemed to do in the past. We know when a myth is just a myth, and we know when we are consciously making an analogy. We know when a dream is a dream, and one hopes we have made at least some strides in being able to distinguish illusion from reality. Even the most ardent Western advocates of mythopoeic approaches today do not and cannot rely on them for explanations. They enrich life, they provide incommunicable mystical and aesthetic experiences, but they do not *explain.*

Nor do metaphors—so essential to poetry—have adequate explanatory powers in relation to the natural world. Although Carolyn Merchant laments the fact that "the 'natural' perception of a geocentric earth in a finite cosmos was superseded by the 'non-natural' commonsense 'fact' of a heliocentric infinite universe,"[13] I would like to think that few ecofeminists doubt the existence of the solar system as we know it today in favor of gender-oriented metaphors. Like it or not, ecofeminists themselves rely very much on science to understand how the biosphere is being polluted and to assess the dimensions of the ecological crisis itself, not on metaphors of "woman = nature."

As for mysticism, its "insights" and "intuitions" are essentially private today, despite the public character they had in the past, when Western consciousness was defined in religious terms. The mystical "insight" that there is a goddess immanent in nature, for example, is ineffable and relies solely on the testimony of faith, which cannot be communicated to anyone who does not share that faith. Ecofeminist mystics may feel a sense of "oneness" and interconnectedness when they "experience 'reclaimed' menstruation; orgasm...and pregnancy, natural childbirth, and motherhood,"[14] but these mystical insights can be communicated neither to men nor to women who do not have such experiences.

I cannot help but note again that if mythopoesis cannot explain the natural world, far less can it explain the human social world. Historically, it has been the responsibility of radical movements to offer an explanation of social realities that challenged the mystifications of hierarchies and ruling classes. Movements have done this by formulating and articulating coherent theoretical understandings of social realities. But ecofeminism reneges on this historical mission of opposition movements when it abjures coherence itself. For ecofeminist Lee Quinby, coherence itself is "totalizing," leads to "polarization," and tends to "become dogma."[15] But to abjure coherence in favor of an "interrogative mode," so typical of postmodernism, is to abjure reason itself, and its project of attempting to give a coherent explanation of the social world. When we lose our rational critical faculties, we lose the basis for political movements themselves—a fact that seems not to trouble Quinby, who does not regard even the loss of the ecofeminist movement—with which she presumably identifies—as a tragedy, being only a "provisional politics." Not only incoherence, but evanescence is now apparently in vogue—in a time when social movements have never been more grimly in need of coherent explanations of social developments today.

Finally, magic is offered as a form of political change. Magic, it should be known, is a primitive and highly instrumental form of analogic technique that tries to ontologically connect symbols—be they words, metaphors, or objects—with what they symbolize. It regards these symbols not merely as representations but as possessing a literally *causal* connection with what is symbolized, as if manipulating a symbol could affect what it symbolizes. An early Neolithic woman who reveres a pregnant-looking female figurine in order to make herself pregnant, for example, performs a form of sympathetic magic, based on the resemblance between the figurine and the pregnancy she would like to attain. Some cultures, to take another example, see a connection between a doll that represents a person and that person. To think that sticking a pin in the doll will harm the person is based on the idea that the resemblance between the doll and the person it symbolizes has an ontological reality, and that there can be a causal relationship between the doll and the person.

Mechanistic science, to be sure, reduced causation to the merely kinetic, and there are certainly forms of causation besides merely physical motion. But magic by its very definition in terms of what we know today ignores any real relationships between causes and effects. It seeks effects essentially without any causes at all. The resemblances between names and what they represent, between invocations and what one is trying to invoke, may certainly be poetic, but they have no causative power. As Gina Blumenfeld once trenchantly noted, such "soothingly simple 'logic-magic' may satisfy

> little children who admonish each other not to step on lines and cracks in the pavement, lest they bring harm to their parents; but when brought to bear on...deeply-entrenched and confusing problem[s], it takes on the character of ingenuous stupidity at best, and at worst, of contemptuous insult. The unfortunate fact remains that such recipes don't undo the double-double think, they merely quadruple the confusion.[16]

Magically "dreaming the dark," cannot affect the realities of domination and power, any more than mythopoesis, and as such, magic cannot be an "art of liberation." It seemed inevitable that Starhawk would have to advise her readers, as she recently did, that "one of the things we learn when we practice magic is that the results don't necessarily happen immediately."[17] In fact, magic *never* works—unless sheer coincidences come into play. Magic may serve very well, however, to addle the minds of people gullible enough to be deceived by the acts of magicians. James Randi, a professional magician, has deliberately performed magical acts that awed his audiences, then shown in painstaking detail how his effects were purely illusory. To claim that magic does work after enough facts exist to show that it is based on trickery is to push back the clock of history not to its Neolithic stage of development, but to the even more distant Pleistocene.

The formalistic scientific reasoning of the 17th century (which many, ecofeminists confuse with reasoning as such) explained the workings of nonhuman nature by looking for the mechanical causes of things—causes capable of accounting for their effects. The claims of this scientific reasoning to be able to explain *everything* in this way—its imperialistic claims to replace all other forms of reasoning—were patently fallacious. When mechanism is attributed to beings and aspects of nature that do not function mechanically, it too ceases to be an explanation and becomes an obscurantist analogy. It was disastrous when mechanistic causation was attributed to all of organic nature and to human society as well.

But the truth is that many parts of nature do in fact function mechanically. There is a mechanical aspect to the movements of the planets, and it is to be hoped that no one would try to fly in an airplane built around a metaphor. Even living organisms have mechanistic aspects, although mechanism cannot in any way account for organic life itself, with all its highly nuanced developmental processes. The elbow functions like a hinge, the shoulder like a ball-and-socket joint. There is a mechanical aspect to the pumping of the human heart.

That mechanistic explanations are inadequate to fully explain the human heart does not belie their truths. Magic and mythopoesis cannot replace clearly valid and tested scientific explanations; nor can they account for those other aspects of nature that are not mechanistic, such as organic life, let alone human society and history. In fact, they do not *explain* anything at all. When mythopoesis and magic are mixed with science for purposes of explanation, the result is not better science; the result is confusion.

We no longer think as earlier peoples thought. We no longer believe that quinces, the hairy fruit, can cure baldness, and we can no longer believe, as people long did, that the earth is an organism.

As Nicholson notes, in terms of scientific explanation, "All the king's horses and all the king's men cannot put Humpty-Dumpty together again"[18]—and neither can the queen's women.

The Problem of Belief

Ecofeminist-theists ask us to do more than sympathetically appreciate the beauty of myths, the importance of mythopoesis and analogy in the history of human consciousness, and the evocative metaphors of poetry. They ask us to *believe* in them, to accept them as descriptions of reality, so that they can become the bases for ethics and politics. They ask us to *believe* that there is literally a goddess immanent in nature. They ask us to *believe* that the earth—or even the cosmos—is literally alive. They ask us to *believe* that women have a special connection with nonhuman nature, that "the authentic female mind is our salvation."[19] They ask us to *believe* that invoking magical words can produce effects in the real world.

But although ecofeminists would like us to believe that there is a goddess immanent in nature, there is not, nor any deity anywhere else. All deities are analogical and metaphorical projections of the human into nature, not anything found in nature itself. As Xenophanes pointed out millennia ago, if horses could paint deities, they would make them look like horses. Although ecofeminists would like us to believe that the earth is an organism, the earth—inasmuch as it includes the inorganic world as well as the organic—is not literally alive, the Gaia hypothesis to the contrary.

The "suprarational" or mythopoeic subjectivities that ecofeminism advocates may not suffice to explain reality, but they may well be effective in getting us to believe things that are not true. Rituals that invoke the goddess do more than simply celebrate the passage of the seasons, cycles of death and rebirth, and the waxing and waning of the moon. They also develop alternative modes of subjectivity that will get us to believe in myths. With hand-clapping, drum-beating, and dance movements, drawing on trances and dreams, the cultic leaders of goddess theology cast spells while congregants are asked to stomp and chant. In goddess theism—as in any religion—the emphasis is on developing the nonrational, for "the mysteries of the absolute can never be explained, only intuited." If it is pointed out that the Enlightenment freed many Western people from such superstitions a long time ago, ecofeminism responds simply by denigrating the Enlightenment itself, instead of dealing with the rational arguments it advanced to remove the supernatural from reality.

All this makes the congregant receptive to unquestioning belief. And belief is, in fact, a central problem in ecofeminist ethics: it depends upon belief in things that are patently untrue. The myths and metaphors and goddesses that ecofeminists ask us to believe in would defy credulity in their own right. But they are even harder to believe when a goddess theologian like Carol P. Christ proceeds to openly announce her own outright agnosticism. Thus, Christ tells us:

> I *imagine,* but I do not know, that the universe has an intelligence, a Great Spirit, that cares as we care...What I do *know* is that whether the universe has a center of consciousness or not, the sight of a field of flowers in the color purple, the rainbow, must be enough to stop us from destroying all that is and wants to be. (emphasis added)[20]

What are we to make of a goddess theologian who deftly reduces her religious beliefs to the aesthetic?

And although Ynestra King believes that "the idea that women are closer to nature is an ideology" and is "not true," she also argues that women can "*consciously choose* not to sever the woman-nature connection" but "use it as a vantage point for creating a different kind of culture and politics." Indeed, King wants ecofeminists to "use the socially-constructed woman equals nature connection to provide an ecological viewpoint, rather than repudiating this construct, like socialist and liberal feminists have done."[21]

But what kind of an ecological "vantage point"—let alone ontological ground for ethics—would that be if it is "not true"? How can this "use" of a "connection" that is "not true" possibly contribute to the project of "recover[ing] ontology as a ground for ethics" and "develop[ing] a different understanding of the relationship between human and nonhuman nature," which King also advocates?[22] How can this ecofeminist, who has long criticized instrumental reason, justify an instrumental "use" of something she believes is not true?

Belief might have been enough to save the dying fairy Tinker Bell in *Peter Pan:* If enough children in the television audience *believed* in her, she would live. But is it possible for intelligent women and men in the 1990s to believe ecofeminist fairy tales without a massive denial of their critical faculties—that is, their ability to reason? To build an ethical system that has as its ground a consciously manipulated falsehood—a patently nonexistent deity, a metaphor of the earth's "aliveness," or mere "social constructions"—defies credulity. When ecofeminism proposes to offer "values" based on the patriarchal tradition that "women = nature"—only to announce that that connection is a mere social construction—we have reached the height of absurdity. Nature was once the ground for ethics because it was *objective*—as distinct from relativistic opinions and passing cultural conventions. Now we are witnessing the reverse: artifacts derived from human culture—sheer conventions, including patriarchal stereotypes as well as myths and goddesses—are being proposed by ecofeminists as the ground for ethics. One would surely have to "think like a mountain" (as Sharon Doubiago asserts "women have always done"[23]) to believe such things—that is, not think at all.

An ethics cannot be based on something that is factually wrong. Much as we may lament the loss of cultural restraints on the market and on technological development in previous eras, we cannot restore those restraints by willfully believing something that we know is not true, especially the mythopoesis, theism, and magic of past cultures. We do know more about the workings of nature than was the case with earlier societies—as ideologically biased as scientific work often is, as much as it has been used to defend privilege, as useful as it has been for capitalism, and as deeply as it magnifies ecological problems. A normative "nature" such as hylozoistic ecofeminists suggest demands that we return to a time when analogy and intuition were the only available alternatives to rational and factually verifiable accounts of the world. To ask people to believe that the earth is an organism, when we know that it is not, is to ask for an abnegation of present human knowledge, and to believe it would depend upon a willed ignorance. It is not a liberatory proposition to live "as if" the earth were alive, when we know that it is not, because that would be to live a lie.

The Return to the Utilitarian

One cannot help but wonder whether it really matters to ecofeminists whether the goddess really exists or not, or whether the earth is really alive or not, or whether women's caring is biological or social. What seems to matter, instead, is that ecofeminist theory and ritual has a poetic, personal value, that it has "resonance," to use popular phraseology. What matters is belief, not truth. Truth, in the ecofeminist firmament, thus becomes a function of expediency. The "woman = nature" connection is true when ecofeminists want it to be true, and it is false when they want it to be false. It is trotted out arbitrarily, when necessary, and denied when necessary. Truth is a matter of whim, whether an ecofeminist has her feet in the Neolithic age of mythopoesis or the modern age of social constructionism—or both.

What is it that has assigned such authority to belief over truth and rationality? The only answer I can give is that what seems to be important to ecofeminists is not the validity of the ideas but their *usefulness* for whatever purposes they may have in mind. The reason we are to believe the myths—the reason we are to accept an ethic grounded in cultural metaphors—is that we are in a state of extreme urgency. Ecofeminist literature—rightly, I might add—abounds with a sense of urgency about the ecological crisis, about the extraordinary rate at which the biosphere is being destroyed. Indeed, it is not only ecofeminists who do this; a series of major ecological disasters, and mass media attention have made the ecological issue a matter of prime concern to people around the world. Clearly, we must do everything we honorably can to address this situation, to prevent the appalling destruction of the ozone layer, to try to reverse the greenhouse effect, to avoid nuclear disaster, to prevent the very fabric of nature—on which we so clearly depend—from being rent irreparably.

But serious questions must be raised about the means that we use to resolve these problems. Presumably, the U.S. government, for example, could do a great deal to save the environment if it put its mind to it. It could shut down factories, severely restrict consumption, set up an environmental police force to make sure no one used Styrofoam cups. In fact, a military dictatorship could take highly efficient steps to end the ecological crisis.

But radical ecologists, obviously, do not advocate such steps. They understand that there are some things that cannot be sacrificed—nor are they in contradiction to an ecological sensibility. Human freedom, for one, is too important to be erased by appealing to the need for ecological stability. That is why most radical ecologists—particularly social ecologists—are committed to grass-roots democracy, to building an independent, anti-capitalist political movement in order to work toward an ecological society. I would argue that another value that must not be sacrificed is a commitment to truth. But when ecofeminists ask us to suspend our disbelief in the supernatural and believe in a goddess, immanent or not, or to believe that nature as such is alive—they are asking us to work toward saving the planet with patent falsehoods. That is, they are asking us to believe these things for purely instrumental reasons—possibly even as an anodyne for our ecological and social anxieties.

Ecofeminism, in effect, has come full circle. By asking us to believe things that are not true for a specific purpose—because they might "work"—it has returned to the very instrumental mode of thinking that the radical ecology movement initially opposed as one of the ideological causes of the ecological crisis. Far from establishing the ground for an ecological ethics—a serious and necessary problem—ecofeminism has succeeded in grounding ethics in a tissue of "social constructions" and asks us to believe they are true, for the purpose of saving the biosphere.

Still another thing that is too precious to be sacrificed, I would argue, is the liberation of women. Reviving metaphors of "women = nature" can be done only at women's expense. Whether it is cultural images or psycho-biological destiny, women are still identified by their traditional, oppressive functions—as the cyclical, the nurturing, and the caring. At a time when most feminists are engaged in a massive struggle to preserve women's right to abortion, ecofeminists are propounding an ideology of the value and even the "sacredness" of life that right-to-lifers could enthusiastically applaud. Indeed, if ecofeminism argues that life is sacred, its logic is to deny women their reproductive freedom. As a result, we find that the very metaphors, symbols, ideals, and images that ecofeminism in all its disparate ways advances could easily turn into an enormous burden on the very women they, as feminists, propose to emancipate.

No movement whose means are instrumental can challenge the instrumentalism of present society. Insofar as "myth" is used for these utilitarian, instrumental purposes, the ecofeminist movement reflects the general society's instrumental, utilitarian and pragmatic orientation. Insofar as it proposes to organize women according to regressive metaphors, it does so once again on the backs of women and participates in the dismal regression that has marked social life over the past few decades.

Playing with Fire

The sacrifice of truth to utility may have unforeseen consequences as well. Cultivating the "suprarational" reaches of mind, imagining oneself to be a "tree"—and allowing that to be "sufficient"—also cultivates a noncritical, anti-intellectual mentality, a mentality that historically has often been a breeding ground for reaction. The prominent culture critic Susan Sontag once warned of a "wing of feminism that promotes the rancid and dangerous antithesis between mind ('intellectual exercise') and emotion ('felt

reality').'' She warned that "precisely this kind of banal disparage-
ment of the normative virtues of the intellect" is "one of the roots
of fascism."[24] Needless to say, ecofeminism is not fascism. But any
philosophy that cultivates emotion at the expense of reason, however well-intentioned, must grapple with the history of the twentieth century.

Unfortunately, some ecofeminists do not seem to have grap-
pled with that history very satisfactorily. For one, Susan Griffin
seems to feel that Nazi ideology was built on a fear of nature. For
example, she maintains that Heinrich Himmler—the head of the
Nazi SS—had the following problem: his "awareness of what
existence is ...was not embedded in the cycle of life."[25] Ironically,
Griffin's choice of Himmler is particularly ingenuous. Heinrich
Himmler was in fact an enthusiastic biocentrist, quite "embedded"
in the cycle of nonhuman life. "How can you find pleasure," he
once wrote in a letter,

> in shooting from behind cover at poor creatures
> browsing on the edge of a wood, innocent,
> defenseless, and unsuspecting? It's really pure
> murder. Nature is so marvelously beautiful, and
> every animal has a right to live...You will find
> this respect for animals in all Indo-Germanic
> peoples. It was of extraordinary interest to me to
> hear recently that even today Buddhist monks,
> when they pass through a wood in the evening,
> carry a bell with them, to make any woodland
> animals they might meet keep away, so that no
> harm will come to them. But with us every slug
> is trampled on, every worm destroyed![26]

Griffin, who has criticized Baconian empiricism on the
grounds that it lacks "self-reflection,"[27] could benefit from a more
empirical study of recent German history. Where she sees Nazi
ideology as identifying Jews with nature, the Nazis in fact saw
themselves as the natural, *völkisch* people and the Jews as cosmo-
politans, representing the Enlightenment and lacking a *Volk*. Such
a gross misinterpretation of recent German history indicates that at

least some prominent ecofeminists are surprisingly ignorant of the potentially reactionary political consequences of irrationalism.

However well-intended many ecofeminists may be, by cultivating the irrational they are playing with fire. Emphases on the irrational have provided a pestilential breeding ground for reaction as well as for romanticism. Indeed, many radical romantics turned into reactionaries partly by mystifying nature and appealing to anti-rational impulses in support of their beliefs. One has only to look at the German *Wandervogel* movement, between the late 19th century and the first quarter of the 20th, to see how many highly idealistic young people, whose views were infused with naturalistic metaphors and whose impulses were largely intuitional, drifted into the Nazi movement of the 1920s and 1930s.[28]

The harsh fact remains that these movements fed into the Nazi propaganda of blood and soil, based on a Germanic *Volk* that was linked to nationalism by a mythos of the "sacred" Germanic earth. That many of these idealistic, anti-capitalist, often anarchistic, and socialistic Germans were absorbed by National Socialism should warn us that irrationalism and mysticism, warming as they may be to the human spirit in a time of social disempowerment, can easily blaze forth like wildfire to consume the great traditions of reason, insight, and democracy that have been handed down to us over the centuries. Ecofeminists must be wary of the fact that their seemingly wholesome spark, borrowed from a mythology of the Neolithic hearth, could potentially sweep many earnest women into a social order that would only deepen their oppression.

The Goddess as a Consumer Item

Insofar as reason—whether instrumental or dialectical—does make distinctions, does divide, does analyze, it is also a *critical* faculty, not simply a means for fragmenting reality. It is a faculty that, far from being prevalent in the English-speaking world today, is in danger of being seriously eroded in an increasingly irrational social reality. The inability of the mythopoeic mentality to make the necessary distinctions between the mythic and the real makes it potentially dangerous, especially in political life. Precisely because myth is nondiscursive and nonrational, precisely because its content is basically vaporous, the future that a specific myth holds out for political life is a wild card in politics. Precisely because it appeals to the nonrational, the use of myth facilitates manipulation.

In our present society, the manipulation of myths, the production and consumption of images, is a dominant activity. In a society obsessed with mere appearances, in which all events are essentially pseudo-events (in Daniel Boorstin's memorable phrase), the goddess and the world-organism are just so many more images, marketed, packaged, and stage-managed. Mythopoesis, as a noncritical faculty, has more potential to support an existing *irrational* social system such as ours than it does to challenge it. Nor need "interconnectedness" and hylozoism lead to economic egalitarianism, as Starhawk dreams; the subjugated have often been encouraged to feel very "interconnected" and "interdependent" on their subjugators, as witness feudal society. Today, capitalism is becoming increasingly stabilized and integrated, the mass media soak up individuality like electronic sponges, the nation-state passes itself off as community, representative government passes itself off as democracy, talk-show hosts pass themselves off as friends, and celebrity gossip passes for intimacy. Today, imagining oneself a tree, "interconnected," and "allowing that to be sufficient," allows one to passively accept the dissolution of the self into an immensely powerful state apparatus, an immensely absorbative economic system, and a frightening resurgence of sexism, racism, homophobia, anti-Semitism, and various ethnic chauvinisms.

The goddess' breast can be a symbol of sustenance—or it can be a symbol of dependency on a consumer culture. The goddess' natural cycles can be a symbol of continuity—or one of doomed fatalistic helplessness in a society pervaded by the market. Appeals to "interconnectedness" and "oneness" may be means to foster our interdependence—or become excuses to suppress dissent and mute genuine class, ethnic, and social differences. "Interconnecteness," too, can be an apt metaphor for the market society itself, in the ebb and flow of financial currency markets across natural boundaries, the balance of trade, the interlocking of individuals into vast corporate and state apparatuses. Our complete reliance on the market for even the most intimate needs reduces us to children who are dependent "on those intricate, supremely sophisticated life-support systems," Christopher Lasch incisively observes, "... and recreates some of the infantile feelings of helplessness"[29] that anodynes like goddess worship may conceal but not remove. Even the hylozoistic analogy can add a certain sheen to capitalist society. Merchant rightly points out that even as views of "living animate nature" died,

> dead inanimate money was endowed with life. Increasingly, capital and the market would assume the organic attributes of growth, strength, activity, pregnancy, weakness, decay, and collapse, obscuring and mystifying the new underlying social relations of production and reproduction that make economic growth and progress possible.[30]

Particularly in our present society—literally glutted with myths and tinsel images—*myth cannot be used to fight myth.* Even if a goddess was worshipped in prehistory, the fact remains that she was always an illusion then, and she is still an illusion now. In an age of manipulation and the tyranny of myth generally, when vast economic and social forces are mobilized to mystify us, we must do everything we can to retain our all-too-fragile rational dimension in politics and develop those critical faculties that hold out a real—not a magical—promise of change.

At a time when American illiteracy rates are skyrocketing, when the educational system is repeatedly on the brink of failing, when the intellectual competence of the American public is generally acknowledged to be at a nadir, and when ignorance of basic facts of history and geography has reached appalling proportions—at such a time it is not surprising that theistic and other appeals to the nonrational are made everywhere, and that the importance of knowledge and the ability to think is minimized. The irrational society of our times is producing irrationality. A mythopoeic sensibility simply obliges us to suspend our rational and critical

faculties and makes us increasingly gullible in dealing not only
with seemingly harmless nostrums but with dangerously reactionary ideas. By appealing to the mythopoeic, those who would use
myth in ecofeminist politics inadvertently foster the public's vul-
nerability to the irrational and sinister trends of our time. As Gina
Blumenfeld once wrote,

> The cultural conditioning which damages us all,
> male and female alike, cannot be undone until we
> gather together all the *human* intelligence we can
> muster, along with our "deep feelings" and
> imagination. The capacity for reflection is not just
> a male prerogative—it is a *uniquely* human
> birthright which must be nurtured and developed
> if we are ever to overcome and heal the splits
> which have brought us to the brink of
> psycholgical, social, and ecological disaster. For
> the fact remains that the violence which has been
> developed and elaborated over centuries of
> domination cannot be uncomplicated—*but if it is
> to be overcome,* it must be opposed with the mode
> of thought and action which is equal to the task.[31]

A moral and healthy ecological and feminist movement must
retain its realism as well as its idealism, in the best sense of the
word. Such a movement surely must provide an ecological ethics,
but not one structured around illusions. It must maintain a firm
sense of the difference between illusion and reality, between the
supernatural and the natural—distinctions for which reason is
necessary. It must address nonhuman nature as it is, not as it once
was or as we fantasize it to be. It must examine society's relationship to nature, not try to dissolve it by considering humans as
merely one of many species. It must remain political and ecological
even as it seeks to become sensuous and caring. In its search for
sensuousness and for emotional alternatives to alienation and
emptiness, it must not lose sight of the crucial importance of reason
by claiming to substitute intuition and myth for scientism and the
mechanization of society. Important as emotions and sensuousness

clearly are, we will pay dearly for the loss of rational political activity. A mystical tendency that indulges our fantasies and subtly renders us captive to a commodified society may eventually, despite its good intentions, help to deprive us of our freedom as individuals and to diminish our activism as social beings.

Historically, the Left has always tried to appeal to the best in people, to their highest moral and intellectual selves. Mind, critical thinking, and intellectuality are precious human attributes that cannot be surrendered without leading to easily manipulated visceral reactions evoked by magic, rituals, and ultimately "responsive leaders" for ends other than freedom. As the Seneca writer John Mohawk has forthrightly put it, "It seems like every time people say they'll do the thinking for you, they fuck you over...I want responsible people, doing the best thinking, not somebody who dreamed something."[32] As the forms of our domination become increasingly sophisticated, it behooves us to boldly "dare to know," in Kant's phrase, rather than to play childish games of "truth or dare."

Chapter 5

Dialectics in the Ethics

of Social Ecology

As a dialectical philosophy, social ecology argues that humanity must be understood *as* the history of humanity, and that nature must be understood *as* the history of nature. Just so, it also argues that science must be understood *as* the history of science. It advances the view that there is much to be gained from examining the role that previous cosmologists played in the development of our own in considering the problem of nature and humanity's relationship to each other, and that earlier peoples in Western culture have asked important questions that our present-day science ignores. In particular, earlier cosmologists addressed and tried to explain—to the best of their ability—at least one very important question that modern science, to its detriment, fails to confront.

This is the fact that, on the one hand, there is order in the natural world, and, on the other hand, that human beings have a rational faculty that is capable of comprehending it in varying degrees. Indeed, the human mind sometimes seems as if it were magnificently developed for understanding the order in the natural world. Just as the world is, at least in part, ordered in a certain way, the human mind is so organized as to be able to comprehend it at various levels of adequacy.

This fact must have struck people in early periods of social development as a remarkable "correspondence." For millennia, they explained the "correspondence" between human reason and the intelligible order in nature by an organismic analogy. The rational human mind could understand the world because the cosmic macrocosm—like the individual microcosm—had a human kind of mind. The various meanings of the Greek word *logos* encompass both the mind's power of comprehension and the fact of the cosmos' comprehensibility. *Logos* referred both to the immanent intelligibility that is discoverable in nature, as well as to the mind that could discover it. This congruency between the rational mind and the rational cosmos explained how thinking can comprehend the world. Hence, the origin of the word "logic" from *logos*. *Logos* also implied the ability to discuss in a rational way, as in dialogues (from the Greek *dia-logos*), how ideas undergo development. Far from defining reason or *logos* as opposed to nature, Socrates, Plato, and Aristotle studied a mind or *nous* that "was always first and foremost mind *in* nature," writes R. G. Collingwood. For Aristotle, as John Herman Randall, Jr., notes, the fact "that men can know their world [was] not a problem, but the most significant fact, both about us and about the world."[1]

This tradition of *logos* was continued through the ancient and medieval periods. On the one hand, it was transformed into a rigid and immutable natural law by the Stoics and Christians. On the other hand, it was perpetuated in its developmental and dialectical form by mystics. With the emergence of modern science, the order of nature seemed open to the human mind in a new form: mathematics. The cosmos was comprehensible and an open book in mathematical terms. But mathematics preserved *logos* in only its most rigid hypothetico-deductive form. Missing from the mathematical *logos* was any ability to explain Aristotle's "most significant fact," or why it was that the now-mathematical cosmos was intelligible to the human mind. It became a merely "metaphysical" question, and the successors of Descartes "abandoned the attempt to prove this correspondence," as Randall observes. Rather, they simply made the assumption that "the order of men's scientific ideas was, in the nature of things, the same as the order of objects in the world," without attempting to justify it metaphysically, philosophically, or cosmologically, let alone scientifically.[2]

Despite science's efficacy in bringing some understanding of nature's operations, "science, in effect, has been permitted to live a lie," writes Murray Bookchin. Science

> has presupposed, with astonishing success, that nature is orderly, and that this order lends itself to rational interpretation by the human mind, but that reason is exclusively the subjective attribute of the human observer, not of the phenomena observed....Science, in effect, has become a temple built on the foundation of seemingly animistic and metaphysical "ruins," without which it would sink into the watery morass of its own contradictions.[3]

Mind was "erected into a second type of substance that served as a ready dumping-ground for everything in experience which physics did not read in mechanical nature," as Randall observes.[4] The qualities of things, like the wetness of water and the coldness of ice, were shoved into this "dumping-ground," as Griffin and other ecofeminists argue. But it was not simply the qualities of things that were so dispensed with. So was the *developmental* causality so typical of organismic life. Self-directiveness and tendency—these too were relegated to the merely subjective, by virtue of their association with the "final causes" of medieval Scholasticism.

Indeed, modern science defined itself most explicitly not by trying to dominate women and nature but by its attack on the Scholastics' "final causes," an issue that constituted perhaps the major battleground between science and Scholastic theology. "To the extent that mechanism became the prevalent 'paradigm' of Renaissance and Enlightenment science," writes Bookchin, "the notion of 'final cause' became the gristmill on which science sharpened its scalpel of 'objectivity,' scientistic 'disinterestedness,' and the total rejection of values in the scientific organon." The backlash against Scholasticism was accompanied by a backlash against organicism generally, in "an exaggerated rejection of all organicism."[5]

In delivering its "sustained polemic," to use Collingwood's phrase, against the Scholastic theory of final causes with its immutable, predetermined teleological ends, early science eliminated any notion that there was any potentiality or nisus in nature to realize implicit forms that have not been fully actualized. In short, mechanistic science, like the putatively organismic approach of many ecofeminists, spilled out the baby with the bathwater. In the course of fighting one extreme, Scholasticism, it moved to another extreme, mechanism.

The mind had become a dumping ground of sorts because mechanism established no intelligible place for mind in the very world that it was describing. The mechanistic worldview and its mathematical *logos* could explain everything, it seemed, except the human mind that perceived it, Descartes' *res cogitans*. The human mind in its Newtonian aspect could not explain organisms organismically; developments, developmentally; history, historically; or society in ways appropriate to human social development. In short, with the mathematical *logos,* the human mind and human society could not be explained intelligibly at all, let alone explain the human ability to comprehend mathematical order. The interface between nature and mind, writes Bookchin, was "replaced by an unbridgeable dualism between mentality and the external world."[6]

Despite the social aim of "mastery over nature," human beings had lost their cosmological place in the mechanistic worldview. Human existence in the scheme of things came to be regarded as a brute accident, and it seemed perfectly sensible for Bertrand Russell in the 20th century to conclude that human life and consciousness are a mere accident in the cosmos, a chance spark in a meaningless world.

This epistemological dualism was accompanied by an ultimately futile attempt to subjugate nonhuman nature by economic and technical forces. Even as Western culture engaged in its *vita activa* to "master" nature and industrial capitalism was developing apace, philosophy remained ensconced in this epistemological dualism. The relationship between nonhuman nature and human nature was cast in largely antagonistic terms, and progress was identified as the technical ability to use nonhuman nature to serve the ends of the marketplace. Human destiny was conceived as the redemption of society from a "demonic" natural world. Writes Bookchin, "The subjugation of human by human...was now celebrated as a common human enterprise to bring nature under human control."[7]

The Problem of Instrumentalism

When the laws of physics, so suitable for understanding inorganic nature, were applied to human society in various scientistic branches of knowledge, the result was to fuel the rise of an instrumental social ethos. Human society does not operate according to physicalist laws; to try to induce it to do so means rendering humanity homogeneous, lifeless, passive, and malleable. This was not simply a matter of ideology. Forces were at work in Western society that stood to make great use of the instrumental ethos that explained people in terms of collections of isolated bodies in eternally lawful motion. For one, the ethos of instrumentalism perfectly suited the emerging nation-state and its unrelenting centralization, bureaucratization, and domination. If people could be reduced to units, they could be manageable and susceptible to administration. If they could be instrumentalized as workers, they could be administered by gigantic corporate entities. The attempt to standardize, instrumentalize, and homogenize the human being as a worker—whether in the bureaucratic state, in the factory, or in the domestic realm—facilitated massive economic exploitation and political domination, despite the attempts of many people to resist this unsavory dehumanizing process.

The instrumental ethos was particularly suited to the needs of capitalism. Capitalism tried to instrumentalize nonhuman nature into raw materials, even as it tried to instrumentalize people as a mere source of labor. As old ethical systems were eroded, the new *homo oeconomicus* who benefited from the exploitation and domination of others blindly followed an established course of self-interest, according to the new "natural laws" that explained economic competition. No longer were individuals integrated into communities that existed to serve a higher purpose. While individuals were liberated from the oppressive "interconnectedness" of traditional and patricentric society, under capitalism they were obliged either to submit to economic "natural laws" or attempt to master them. Again, this is not merely a matter of ideology; in a market society, it is everyday reality. If the instrumental ethos reduced moral purpose to self-interest in order to survive, capitalism made competition a social imperative. Only mastery of the economic process could assure the self-preservation of the individual capitalist and his enterprise in the all-consuming competitive marketplace.

Ultimately, women in the domestic realm were also to be largely homogenized. As the domestic realm became increasingly reduced to the isolated nuclear family, women's household duties came to be analyzed and prescribed in increasing detail. Despite 19th-century women's cultural "mission" as bearers of morality in the "cult of true womanhood," home economics in the domestic realm was integral to the competitive economics of the marketplace, producing and educating children and administering the household along increasingly rationalized lines. Women's participation in the "caring" professions—of nursing, social work, and others—was necessary to the system for "cleaning up after the men," just as women's childbearing and childrearing were necessary to produce workers for capitalism.

But capitalism did not simply try to transform human and nonhuman nature into raw materials. It also tried to commodify nearly every aspect of human existence, to ensure the dependence of both the public and the domestic spheres on the market. This process ruptured any organic integration between human and nonhuman communities. In this century, everything from transportation and communication, to courtship and reproduction have been subject to commodification. As such, commodification "hollowed out" whatever sense of ethical purpose and meaning of life had been inherited from the past. The recently liberated "individual" became a mere shell of a self. As Max Horkheimer wrote,

> we have on the one hand the self, the abstract ego
> emptied of all substance except its attempt to
> transform everything in heaven and on earth into
> means for its preservation, and on the other hand
> an empty nature degraded to mere material, mere
> stuff to be dominated, without any other purpose
> than that of this very domination.[8]

Most important for the purposes of the present discussion, reason itself fell victim to the very instrumental ethos that it had helped foster. "Gone is the cosmos with whose immanent *logos* my own can feel kinship, gone the order of the whole in which [humans have their] place," writes Hans Jonas.[9] No longer was the *logos* of the world embedded in an ethical cosmos. No longer addressing ends, reason was reduced to an instrumental means. Neither personal nor social freedom has roots any longer in the objective world, but merely exist in the eyes of the beholder, a function of public opinion rather than objective reality. What we think of as reason today is reason reduced to a mere "skill" or instrument, to a mere means to attain self-interested ends. For instrumental reason, it makes no difference whether its statements are designed to justify women's claims to reproductive freedom or validate racist neo-Nazi claims. Its sole job is to determine whether these claims—or any claim—are logically consistent, not whether they are morally right or wrong. "Rightness" and "wrongness" themselves are merely values or even social constructions that each person may accept or reject, depending upon his or her opinion or needs. In themselves, they have no standing in presumably morally neutral logical operations. It is this kind of thinking that the 1960s counterculture—long before ecofeminists appeared on the scene—regarded as "linear."

Guided by operational standards of logical consistency and pragmatic success, reason was "validated exclusively by its effectiveness in satisfying the ego's pursuits and responsibilities. It makes no appeal to values, ideals, and goals." In politics and ethics, reason was "denatured," as Bookchin has pointed out, "into a mere methodology for calculating sentiments—with the same operational techniques that bankers and industrialists use to administer their enterprises."[10] It became an instrument for advancing personal interests to achieve individual ends—and not for *defining* those ends. Worse, it became an instrument for administering human beings—not for defining and formulating an ethically meaningful existence. Science's "'value-free,' presumably ethically 'neutral' methodology" allows instrumentalism to remain ideologically secure. "If we mistrust reason today," writes Bookchin,

> it is because reason has enhanced our technical powers to alter the world drastically without providing us with the goals and values that give these powers direction and meaning. Like Captain Ahab in Melville's *Moby Dick,* we can cry out forlornly: "All my means are sane; my motives and objects mad."[11]

But instrumental reason has been fallaciously criticized as if it constituted reason per se rather than just one form of reason. Here again, the baby is spilled out with the bathwater. As we shall see, there are *other* forms of reason that are not hypothetico-deductive, instrumental, and formalistic in character.

To see science as "dominating" in itself obscures the much more insidious process of the instrumentalization of society, and the social forces that have benefited so greatly from their use of instrumental techniques. This one-sided view leads inevitably to the conclusion that science and reason—*rather than these social forces*—are the problem. Ecofeminist Corinne Kumar d'Souza criticizes science for its "universalism,"[12] and to be sure, scientific claims have certainly been grossly overstated. When applied to human societies, for example, whether Western or non-Western, science has more often facilitated social manipulation than not and has thus played a role in restricting human freedom. Indeed, it is questionable that a science of society, or sociology, can ever explain in the human world what physical science is expected to rigorously explain in the inorganic world.

But d'Souza, in her understandable struggle to defend the integrity of non-Western cultures from the devastation of Western-style development, seems to reject science itself. Like many ecofeminist theories, this too amounts to pouring out the baby with the bathwater. That science has made imperialistic claims does not require that we reject science as such. Rather, it places upon us the challenging responsiblity of putting science in its proper context (as an explanation of the subject matter with which it can adequately deal), to understand that it is inadequate to explain everything, and to seek more encompassing modes of explanation.

By confusing science with the imperialistic ideology called *scientism*, ecofeminists like d'Souza dismiss the extent to which physical science is quite simply true in its own sphere of competence. That physics does not supply adequate explanations of biological development, let alone human development, does not negate its presuppositions and insights even in building houses and bridges. Even hunting-gathering peoples use instrumental reason when they build shelter or get food, as Bookchin points out: "We can no more divest ourselves of instrumental reason than we can divest ourselves of technics."[13] Science provides a much better explanation of mechanistic processes that affect all organisms and human cultures in the biosphere—like the operations of the solar system and the functioning of the heart—than does metaphor.

An Evolutionary Perspective

Science, as we have noted, *is* the history of science. Just as mechanism has a delimited place—even in organic life and human society—so do analogy and development. Analogy, as I have noted earlier, plays an important role in biological sciences concerned with form. Biomechanics studies analogies between technologies and biological phenomena. In organic evolutionary science, evidence that evolution has occurred rests at least partly on comparative anatomy and embryology. All vertebrates develop with surprising similarities, for example. Closely related groups of organisms have like structures and functions.

If science uses analogy, science in the overall also reveals a developmental picture, whether it understands itself as doing so or not. For example, a chemist knows that two atoms of hydrogen and one atom of oxygen will always produce water (at least on the terrestrial level). This is an immutable chemical fact. But placed in the context of the development of the inorganic universe, that chemical combination occupies a certain *historical* place. According to the generally accepted big-bang theory, all of the matter and energy in the universe was once concentrated very densely into a tiny volume at a very high temperature. This primeval "fireball" exploded, resulting in an expansion that continues today. Neutrons and protons formed from their quark constituents. In nanoseconds, some of the hydrogen was converted into helium. The expanding universe thinned and cooled enough to condense into individual galaxies and then stars, leading to the present universe. Gravity collapsed the matter into the celestial objects such as we see now. The billions of galaxies in the universe are all receding from each other at speeds comparable to that of light. After a very long time, the solar system, including the earth, was formed. Somewhere in the course of this development, oxygen was formed from "primal" hydrogen and combined with it to form water. Here we see a striking example of a cumulative inorganic evolution: the "natural history of water," as it were. Water was not present in the hot fireball; rather, it is the product of a development in inorganic evolution. Although its chemical formation is subject to natural law, it has a natural history.

When scientists look for alternative explanations to mechanistic natural law, they often turn to randomness. And indeed, to the best of our knowledge, randomness is at work in the universe—although chaos theory has recently been finding mathematical order even in chaos. But when one looks over the course of the development of the universe—from fireball to galaxies to planets to the "nutrient broth" of amino acids to unicellular life to plants, animals, and human society—it is hard to attribute it exclusively to randomness, despite the fact that there were many random events. Its zigs and zags and dead ends notwithstanding, a directionality is apparent in the evolution of the cosmos. Looking back in retrospect, this is simply a fact—not a mere hypothesis—and must be philosophically accounted for. Indeed, both organic and inorganic nature literally develop. The word evolution is correctly applied to both: to inorganic evolution, concerned with the development of the physical universe from unorganized uniformity, as well as to organic evolution, concerned with the development of animals and plants by a process of continuous change and differentiation from previously existing forms.

This is not to say that inorganic or organic evolution *had* to develop in the specific directions they did. Nor is it to say that the history of the cosmos had to lead inevitably from the hot fireball to human society. We do not know if the origination of life in its present forms was inevitable; nor can we say that the organic development that did occur was predetermined. The earth is a microspeck in the infinite universe, and human evolution as we know it may be one form of development among many others in the "tree" of evolution. But like it or not, a very distinct development *did* take place and has to be *explained.* It cannot be dissolved into mere contingency or fantasies about what might or might not have occurred. Moreover, we must ask not merely *how* it occurred, but *why* it occurred, whether it reveals any rationale or is merely a meaningless flow of random events. When all is said and done, this natural history clearly *reveals* ever greater differentiation of life-forms, increasing subjectivity and flexibility, and finally the emergence of intellectuality, intentionality, and a high order of choice, which forms a precondition for freedom.

To labor over whether this was inevitable is to make a meaningful problem meaningless. We must inquire into the *kind* of development that led to the emergence of existing species, including the human, with its conscious willfulness, enormous powers of conceptual thought, symbolic language, and well-organized but highly mutable social institutions. To dodge this question, to regard human evolution as a pure accident, as Stephen Jay Gould does in his recent book *Wonderful Life* (based on the many exotic early life-forms fossilized in the Burgess Shale), is to place a veil of obscurity over the very real, existential evolution of life from a simple, unicellular organism through increasingly neurologically complex life-forms, to large-brained animals, and to a highly self-conscious creature called *homo sapiens.* The failure to try to deal rationally with this evolution, whose history has also literally been "carved in stone" by the fossil remains of the past is to sidestep profound philosophical questions that have very important ethical implications.

One aspect of inorganic and organic evolution that has reflected a remarkable interaction of persistence and change is subjectivity. Subjectivity is not unique to human beings; it too has a natural history of its own. From its most rudimentary forms in unicellular organisms, as mere self-identity and sensitivity, it has expanded throughout natural history. The earliest, simplest organisms that developed had self-identity—even if only as the mere metabolic activity on the part of an amoeba to *actively* persist and reproduce itself in an environment that would otherwise tend to dissolve it. Although seemingly unconscious—indeed, perhaps even incapable of consciousness—the very fact that it is busy maintaining itself is a germinal form of selfhood and a nascent form of subjectivity. Whatever else an amoeba may have, this active self-identity distinguishes it from the nonliving environment in which it is immersed.

> Natural history includes a history of mind as well as of physical structures—a history of mind that develops from the seemingly "passive" interactivity of the inorganic to the highly active cerebral processes of human intellect and volition. This history of what we call "mind" is cumulatively present not only in the human mind but also in our bodies as a whole, which largely recapitulate the expansive development of life-forms at various neurophysical levels of evolution....What we today call "mind" in all its human uniqueness, self-possession, and imaginative possibilities is coterminous with a long evolution of mind.[14]

Mind thus derives as a form of a broad evolution of subjectivity, in the course of the cumulative development of increasingly complex forms. In this sense, human subjectivity is "the very history of natural subjectivity, not merely its product."[15]

Ecofeminism has no such graded evolutionary approach to nature. It either sees "nature" as a social construction, or as an effusive undifferentiated "oneness." Social ecology opens an entirely different approach to a definition of nature and to the reconciliation of humanity with the natural world. This approach is what Murray Bookchin calls dialectical naturalism.

Dialectical Naturalism

What, then, do social ecologists mean by dialectical naturalism?[16]

Dialectical naturalism is an attempt to grasp nature as a developmental phenomenon, both in its organic and social realms. All organic phenomena change and, even more important, undergo development and differentiation. They form and re-form, while actively maintaining their identity until, barring any accident, they fulfill their potentialities. But since the cosmos, seen in an overview of its evolution, is developmental as well, dialectical naturalism approaches the world as a whole from a developmental perspective. Its various realms—inorganic, organic, and social—are distinct from each other, and yet they grade into one another.

This approach above all focuses on the transitions of a developing phenomenon, which emerge from its potentiality to become fully developed and self-actualized. These transitions, in turn, arise from a process of "contradiction" between a thing as it is, on the one hand, and a thing as it potentially should become, on the other.

As a result of a developmental transition, each new potentiality in a development cumulatively contains all its previous phases, albeit transformed, even as it itself—when it is fully actualized—contains the potentiality to become a new actuality. The emergence of life out of inorganic nature is such a transition. Life not only emerges from the inorganic, but it contains the inorganic within itself, yet it is clearly *more* than the inorganic. Together, inorganic and organic nature constitute what social ecology calls "first nature." The emergence of human society out of first nature, in turn, is also such a transition, for society contains the vast evolution of its biological heritage within itself, yet goes beyond biological evolution as such to become what we would rightly call social evolution. This social evolution is thus what social ecology calls "second nature"—a phrase that is meant to emphasize the *natural* continuity between biological and social evolution.

To give another example of this process of development that incorporates a previous development from which it stemmed into itself: a human adult does not simply replace the child he or she once was. Rather, the child is absorbed into and is developed beyond the state of childhood and, barring accidents, is hopefully actualized into a fuller, more differentiated being. This development follows a logic that is cumulative, that contains not only the child's biological course of growth but his or her social development as well.

In examining the process of development, dialectical naturalism is especially interested in *form* and the way it is organized in inorganic and organic nature. From formal ensembles, tensions or "contradictions" emerge. Contradiction in dialectical naturalism—as in all dialectical thought—is a dynamic process that impels self-development. But unlike other dialectical approaches, which have regarded contradictions as abstractly logical or as narrowly materialistic, dialectical naturalism "conceives contradiction as distinctly natural."[17]

In an organism, for example, there is a tension between what that organism could potentially be when it is fully actualized, on the one hand, and what it is at any given moment before that development is fulfilled. That which it is *constituted to become or "should be"*—the implicit—causes that which it *is*—its immediate explicit existence at a given moment in its development—to be unstable.

> A thing or phenomenon in dialectical causality
> remains unsettled, unstable, in tension—much as
> a fetus ripening toward birth "strains" to be born
> because of the way it is constituted—until it

> develops itself into what it "should be" in all its
> wholeness or fullness. It cannot remain in endless
> tension or "contradiction" with what it is
> organized to become without becoming warped
> or undoing itself. It must ripen into the fullness
> of its being.[18]

This instability of contradiction propels a being toward self-development, whatever it should become by virtue of they way its potentialities are constituted. To use the example of human development again, given the potentiality of a child to become an adult, there is a tension that exists between infancy, childhood, adolescence, and youth, until the child's abilities are fully actualized as a mature being. To be sure, its development may be arrested or warped during any one of these transitional phases, which obviously leaves it less than a fully actualized—or in a sense a less than rational—even "irrational"—human being. (The same can be said to apply to society.) Accordingly, impelled by a logic of growth (a process that has its mechanico-chemical aspects, to be sure, in chromosomes and the creation of proteins from nucleic acids), development occurs, yet preserves the old. This cumulative approach produces a continuum "that contains the entire history of [a child's] development."[19]

Thus, dialectical naturalism does not attempt to efface a dualism like the dualism of mind and body, for example, simply by trying to collapse mind into body, as some ecofeminists seem to do. Although Western culture—especially in recent centuries—has conceived of mind and body as radically separated from each other, we cannot "heal" this split by reducing the one to the other. A human body without mind can hardly be called conscious. In fact, the mind-body dualism has a basis in an ontological *duality.* Mind does emerge out of body as something distinct, even as it is part of and remains embedded in the body. Indeed, it is a socially conditioned but organic *differentiation* of the body's own development, as the evidence of evolution shows us. A dialectical naturalist approach overcomes mind-body dualism not by rejecting the distinction between the two but by articulating the continuum along which the human mind has evolved. The relationship between mind and body—their distinctness, as well as mind's dependence on and its origins in first nature alike—is a *graded* phenomenon, as Bookchin has argued, not one in which mind and body are rigidly separated.

Nor is dialectical naturalism a macrocosm-microcosm "correspondence theory." Indeed, development in inorganic nature has not been of precisely the same kind that we find in organic nature. We can explain many biological facts by means of chemistry, Bookchin has pointed out, but we cannot explain chemical facts by means of biology. The history of inorganic nature is a development of reactivity and interactivity, in which increasingly complex forms arise from interactions of elementary particles. The history of organic nature is a fully active development, in which—however nascently—even the simplest unicellular organic forms are busily involved in maintaining their self-identity from dissolving into their inorganic environment, even as they absorb the substances they need for their self-maintenance from that immediately contiguous environment. In the evolution of life-forms, nascent self-identity developed into more complex subjectivity and form, and ever-greater self-intentionality emerged in maintaining themselves, in modifying their environment, and in rendering that environment more habitable—an elaboration of the self-identity that distinguishes organic from inorganic development. Yet despite this increasing subjectivity and intentionality of organisms, an evolutionary continuity remains between inorganic and organic nature, and at the roots of the intentionality of complex organisms we find the increasingly complex formal arrangements of inorganic particles and compounds. There is wisdom in the claim of 18th-century Enlightenment thinkers like Denis Diderot that the differences between the inorganic and organic worlds—and between different organisms—lie in what he called "the organization of matter."

Dialectical naturalism, it goes without saying, sees development as immanent in nature itself. First nature alone, in all its wholeness, richness, self-creativity, and marvelousness requires no supernature to explain its processes. Unlike Hegelian dialectics, with its recourse to "Spirit," dialectical naturalism does not posit the presence of a spiritual principle apart from nature's own self-evolving attributes to explain either inorganic or organic existence. Nor does it posit any "Absolute," as Hegelian dialectics did, in which development is completely fulfilled. Rather, in dialectical naturalism, self-directiveness remains a tendency whose fulfillment, while marked by ever-greater degrees of "wholeness," remains open-ended and continually self-formative.

Dialectical reasoning is a form of reasoning that attempts to understand the developmental processes in first and second nature that I have been describing. It clearly differs from instrumental reason, which freezes a phase of a development in order to analyze its components. That physiology and anatomy can satisfactorily analyze a human body only if they regard it as fixed and unchanging should be fairly obvious, even though a living body is continually developing and differentiating. Without operating on this level of fixity, to be sure, we would know nothing about the structure and functions of the human organism, a knowledge that is indispensable for the details of medical diagnosis and therapy. Analysis, in effect, can indeed provide a great deal of knowledge about things. But instrumental or analytical reason cannot explain the developmental, because developmental processes involve more than simply the rearrangement of component parts into a new arrangement. Development involves a transition from one state of being to another for which mere analysis provides only a woefully incomplete account. Dialectical reasoning, indeed, absorbs analogical and analytical forms of reasoning in its developmental approach but goes far beyond them.

Dialectical reasoning originated in the *logos* concept of the Greeks. Having survived in various forms over the millennia, it blossomed in the 19th-century German Enlightenment and was elaborated most fully in its time by Hegel.[20] For Hegel, dialectical reasoning conceives of basic, seemingly contradictory logical categories—like "being" and "nothing"—as leading to the category of "becoming," a category that dialectical logic takes as its great point of departure and also begins to define becoming for what it really is, namely development. Becoming, with its full wealth of logically

educed categories, in Hegel's logical works, is literally the cumulative history of pure thought. Dialectical reasoning describes processes of cumulative change in which the logically prior is partly
annulled, incorporated, and transcended by its synthesis as a new
category.

In everyday commonsensical thinking, it might seem difficult
to believe that a consistent developmental logic could be produced
that had the rigor that reason has generally claimed for itself. But
despite certain limitations, the logical works of Hegel demonstrate
that this can be done with extraordinary brilliance. What Hegel did
was to try to systematically understand the nature of becoming, to
resolve "the paradox of a 'something' that 'is' and is simultaneously
developing into 'what is not.'" He took the vast array of logical
categories that had surfaced in Western philosophy, including
many of his own, and arranged them from the simplest to the most
complex in an order in which each was educed from its own
internal logic and incompleteness to its sucessor, filling out the rich
terrain of thought in a cumulative, increasingly differentiated, and
ever more adequate approximation of a rational whole.

Hegel referred to the potentiality of a logical category as that
which is implicit, or *an sich,* and to the more developed, explicit
category emerging from it as the explicit, or *für sich.* He designated
the rational fulfillment of a potentiality as its actualization (*an und
für sich*). Owing to its incompleteness or "contradictory" nature in
the elaboration of the "whole," the implicit strives, in a sense, to
fulfill itself by its own developmental logic, the way living forms
in nature "strive" to grow and develop by a tension between what
they are at any given moment and what they should be in their
maturity. The process by which the implicit becomes explicit is
rendered in Hegelian terminology by the untranslatable German
word *Aufhebung,* sometimes expressed as "transcendence" or
"sublation." In an *Aufhebung,* the new category or phase of a
development "contradicts" or "negates" the previous one, even as
it incorporates it in a more complete condition. It should be
emphasized that *contradiction* in dialectical reason does not refer
to a contradiction between two arbitrarily chosen statements that
have no developmental relationship to each other. Rather, dialec-

tical contradiction involves the fulfillment of a potentality that negates the previous state, absorbs it, and goes beyond it—not the juxtaposition of ideas or facts that patently have no connection with each other.

Dialectical reasoning uses neither the inductive process of empiricism nor the hypothetico-deductive process of formal reason but a third form of thinking that Bookchin calls *eduction.* Eduction, writes Bookchin, is directed "toward an exploration of [a potentiality's] latent and implicit possibilities." It aims to understand the *inherent logic* of a thing's development—that is, the point from which it started, where it is now, and where by its immanent developmental logic it should go. Eduction attempts to render "the latent possiblities of a phenomenon fully manifest and articulated." Dialectical premises are not random hypotheses but rather potentialities that stem from a distinct continuum, with a past, present, and latent future of their own. From these potentialities is educed a graded differentiation toward wholeness—without dissolving the richly articulated phases that make up the whole into a vague, unarticulated "oneness."

In its Hegelian form, dialectics operates primarily within the realm of thought. Hegel's system invokes an inexplicable cosmic spirit *(Geist)* that culminates in a mystical Absolute. Marxian dialectics, in turn, as developed by Frederick Engels, tilts toward the relatively mechanistic science of the 19th century, which dealt more with matter and motion than with a truly organic development. In contrast to both of these, dialectical *naturalism* is completely informed by ecology. Development remains strictly naturalistic, without recourse to Hegel's spirit or to Frederick Engels' mechanical kinetics. Nor does the naturalistic dialectics advanced by Bookchin terminate in an Absolute, or any notion of an "end of history." It thus remains more open-ended, fluid, spontaneous, organic, and free from predeterminations than we find in the dialectical tradition by which it is informed.

In first and second nature, the character of dialectical development varies from the evolution of the inorganic and organic to the evolution of human society. But the very fact of the evolution of the organic out of the inorganic, and of the social out of the

organic (each preserving what rationally came before it in a transformed state) dialectically grounds second nature in first nature
itself. Dialectical naturalism is thus both a form of reasoning and
an ontological form of causality.

As both a form of reasoning and as an account of development
in first and second nature, dialectical naturalism offers an explanation for Aristotle's "most significant fact," with which we opened
this chapter: the fact that the world of nature is comprehensible to
the human mind. It is because human beings are a product of the
increasing subjectivity in first nature—not created by God, not a
microcosm that "corresponds" to an analogical macrocosm—that
they can understand the processes of first nature. Human beings
and human society evolved out of first nature—even as they remain
part of it and are embedded in it. By virtue of the very "physical
anthropology" of human mentality, human subjectivity is
grounded in first nature, as a product of its emergence, and therefore can comprehend it.

The Ethics of Social Ecology

A rationality that conceives reality as the actualization of
potentialities into ever-differentiating degrees of wholeness has
profound ethical implications. Obviously, the ground of an ecological ethics must be ontological: it cannot be grounded in the
vagaries of social constructions, public opinion, or tradition, much
less in patently absurd myths. In social ecology, nature reenters the
philosophical and political sphere of Western culture as an ontological ground for ethics. This ethics is one that is premised on
natural evolution and the emergence of second nature out of first
nature.

As we have seen, first nature's development is inorganic, then
(in our planetary biosphere, at least) biological. Subjectivity increasingly emerges from the most nascent unicellular process of
self-maintenance and subjectivity, through the rudimentary
choices exercised by highly flexible mammals, to the elementary

conceptual thought of advanced primates. Here, as we have seen, is a graded development of subjectivity in the evolution of life.

Yet animal behavior is for the most part determined by biology. Although ethnologists commonly speak of "animal societies" with impunity, animals do not have the unique type of community structures developed by humans. Their "social arrangements," as Bookchin has argued, such as those of ants, are genetically programmed, even though the role of the genetic is lessened as we approach primate forms of life.

With humanity, natural evolution gives rise to social evolution in the fullest sense of the word. While we are embedded in first nature, we have also evolved from it into something different in very important ways. If "being determines consciousness," so to speak, for animals, it is by no means strictly true for human beings, Marxian theory notwithstanding. Human beings create *institutions* that are often highly mutable, indeed subject to radical and revolutionary changes, a phenomenon that does not appear in animal communities. The evolution of society, which uniquely characterizes humans, gives them the ability to change their social relations in a great variety of ways, potentially toward ever greater self-consciousness and freedom. This represents a development from mere animal community to human society, a crucial advance, however phased it may be, from the world of the biological to the social, from first nature to second nature.

Unlike animals, human beings can clearly perceive that a society is destroying the biosphere, and they can try to do something about it. Unlike animals, humans also engage in struggles to make changes in their lives and in their social institutions. With their highly developed nervous systems and brains, they are the only animals with minds that seem capable of sophisticated conceptual reason and a richly symbolic vocabulary that forms the basis for highly intricate modes of thinking and human consociation. And unlike other animals, humans are able to make *moral* choices. They are potentially ethical creatures that can, for example, impart "rights" not only to themselves but even to nonhuman life-forms if they so choose. Second nature thus marks a new evolutionary phase of nature, with its sociality, institutions, intellectuality, language, ethics, and political life.

We know only too well from the history of civilization, however, that human society has not as yet reached its full maturity, rationality, or indeed, its full humanity. Dialectics, by exploring the potentiality and internal logic of a development, educes what society *should be.* This is not an arbitrary endeavor. It must be validated by reason and by real material as well as cultural possibilities. By examining what potentialities humans have as they grade out of first nature, social ecology advances the ethical view that their capacities will not be realized unless they create a rational ecological society based on an ethics of complementarity with first nature. But what society *should be* is vastly different from what it *is.* Where it should be rational and ecological if humanity's potentialities are fulfilled, it is irrational and anti-ecological today. This potentiality, the "should be," becomes in the ethics of social ecology, the overarching standard of actualization and wholeness. Herein lies the *critical* thrust of social ecology's ethics: the fact that by educing the true actualization of humanity's potentialities, it provides a standard by which we may judge the irrationality of the "what is"—not mere appeals to the vagaries of myth and religion.

There remains still another step, or *Aufhebung,* that must be made in natural and social evolution. This is the step that transforms second nature—with all its marvelous advances and its terrible abuses—into a "synthesis" of first and second nature in the form of a harmonious, conscious, and ecological "free nature." In free nature, both human and nonhuman nature come into their own as a rational, self-conscious, and purposeful unity. Humanity, as a product of natural evolution, brings its consciousness to the service of both first and second nature. It brings its consciousness to the service of first nature by diminishing the impact of natural catastrophes, and promoting the thrust of natural evolution toward diversity and ending needless suffering, thereby fueling the creativity of natural evolution through its technics, science, and rationality. In free nature, we would no longer expect human beings to regard themselves as the lords of creation but as conscious beings, indeed as the products of natural evolution, in the rich ecological mosaic of an ecocommunity. There, human needs and the needs of nonhuman life-forms would be joined in a complementary way so that there is a beneficial, reciprocal relationship between the two. In this truly mutualistic free nature, humanity would cease to be divided against the nonhuman world—and against itself. Indeed, in free nature, human society would be nonhierarchical and cooperative. Society's "completeness" would be based on the "completeness" of humans in their self-fulfillment as rational, free, and self-conscious beings.

Free nature's end is hardly a predetermined "final cause" in a Scholastic sense, nor a predetermined course of social evolution. There is no certainty that society will become free and rational and thereby ecological. The potentiality of society to develop into its fullness is immanent but not inevitable. Today our *conceptions* of freedom have never been so fully elaborated, but it requires a supreme act of consciousness, as Bookchin emphasizes, to achieve a free world. Since we have not attained this free nature, human beings still remain in the perverted development of second nature, and first nature is still being grievously harmed. But we can certainly advance a vision of "free nature" as an ethical "should be" that alone would mark the fruition of nature's and humanity's potentialities, and we can seek to develop an ethics of complementarity, even as we fight to destroy hierarchy in society. It is the end, the telos, so to speak, albeit by no means a predetermined one, toward which we strive to fulfill both ourselves and first nature.[21]

The ethics of social ecology has particularly profound implications for women. As human beings, women's lives are no more determined by biology than are men's. Unlike other female animals, the human female is capable of making decisive choices about when and under what circumstances she will reproduce. The distinction between the facile ethical proposals of ecofeminists and social ecology's ethics should be especially clear on the issue of abortion and reproductive freedom generally. An ethical prescription superficially drawn from first nature which argues that all life is sacred would, if its adherents are to be consistent, oblige us to oppose abortion on the grounds that it is destructive to "life". By contrast, in social ecology's ethics, in which first nature is a realm of increasing subjectivity out of which society emerges, women would have a right to reproductive freedom that is grounded in the emergence of society and natural evolution. As human beings uniquely capable of making ethical choices that increase their freedom in the context of an ecological whole, women's reproductive freedom would be a given.

Women and men share a common natural history. As Chiah Heller has pointed out, women's nature is also human nature, and as such, is grounded in organic evolution. The human capabilities for reason, consociation, and ethical behavior are as female as they are male.

> The unifying principles within human nature...constitute a common natural history shared by both men and women;...Foremost, woman, as the female expression of human nature, shares with man the capacity to build a "second nature." This second nature includes the distinctly human potential to create cultural institutions, a written language, and the capacities for rational thought, intellectual mentation, and self-conscious reflection. The first answer to the "woman question" must be that woman represents a distinctive expression of second nature: a nature which is the realization of the potential for self-consciousness in "first nature."... When feminists focus exclusively on woman's difference from man...we forget to appreciate that which makes female *human nature* distinctive.[22]

In reality, as distinguished from patriarchal mystifications, men and women are not ontological "opposites." They are, in fact, *differentiations* in humanity's potentiality to achieve a rich variegated wholeness. Maleness and femaleness in human beings is a transformation, an *Aufhebung,* of male and femaleness in animals, inasmuch as gender traits are radically more malleable in human beings than they are in nonhuman male and female organisms.

Human beings, by virtue of their potentiality to choose different social roles, transcend the more rigidly biological sexual differences among nonhuman beings. The emergence of second nature thus initiates a new dialectic in which men and women can have interchangeable roles in all realms of human life without losing their sexual distinctiveness. That women and men today can potentially do so at a high level of social integration is truly an evolutionary advance

If it is true that "men make their own history, but they do not make it...under circumstances of their own choosing," as Marx once said, neither do women. Without a dialectical, evolutionary view of nature, ecofeminism will succeed only in integrating itself into existing society with trendy metaphors of "interconnectedness" and "aliveness" and an appeal to the irrational rather than the best faculties we possess. If it follows the muddy direction created by ecofeminism, it will regress into a mentality where choice is replaced by tradition, will by ritual, insight by the incantations of priestesslike leaders, and psychologically regress to a time when humanity was guided more by the canons of tribalistic blood-ties than by the humanistic association of thinking citizens. With an ecological ethics grounded in the potentiality of human beings to consciously and rationally create a free ecological society, we can begin to develop an ecological political movement that challenges the existing order on the grounds that it denies both humans and nonhumans their full actualization. To meet that challenge, we need the best faculties we have—our knowledge of nature, and the understanding of what we should be—rather than regressive myths of "oneness" that carry us back to a past we should have long outgrown.

Chapter 6

Women in Democratic Politics

In the ideology of the 19th-century "cult of true womanhood," middle-class white women were given the role of maintaining the family home as a moral sanctum while their entrepreneur husbands pursued their competitive commercial lives in the stormy outside world. Even as "women's sphere"—the domestic realm—was becoming increasingly rationalized by "home economics," women were expected to have a moral mission of preserving the home as a realm of caring and nurturing. Women were obliged to stay out of extradomestic affairs—whether political or economic—and become guardians of the home as the human heart of society. Insofar as they were permitted to emerge from the domestic realm, it was to do "women's work" such as social work and nursing.

Like that 19th-century ideology, ecofeminism, too, sees "home" as "woman's sphere," whether as a social construction or as a matter of biology. They note that the word "ecology" derives from the Greek word *oikos,* which means "home." "What has been traditionally thought of as 'woman's sphere,'" writes Judith Plant, is "home and its close surroundings." Although Plant believes the home is "women's sphere" for social and not biological reasons, "home is the theater of our human ecology," where "the real work is." Indeed, "home" is the "source of our human-ness," she writes, and the locus of what she calls "women's values." Catherine Keller, too, emphasizes the connection between "home" and ecology: she considers that "to be simply at home again, in our bodies, our

131

worlds, is to become ecocentric: 'eco,' from *oikos,* the Greek word
for 'home.' "[1]

Unlike the 19th-century ideology, however, most
ecofeminists do not seek to literally confine women to the domestic
sphere in the sense of *oikos* as "the household." Rather, they seek
to extend the very concept of "women's sphere" as home to embrace
and absorb the the community as a whole. Writes ecofeminist
Cynthia Hamilton, "women are more likely than men to take on
[community] issues *precisely* because the home has been defined
and prescribed as a woman's domain." (emphasis added)[2] Thus,
one of the keystones of ecofeminist analysis is that the home and
community—as the locus of ecological struggle—is particularly
relevant to women. Citing community activists like Lois Gibbs at
Love Canal, ecofeminists Diamond and Orenstein argue that in
industrialized countries,

> Women who are responsible for their children's
> well-being are often more mindful of the
> long-term costs of quick-fix solutions. Through
> the social experience of caretaking and nurturing,
> women become attentive to the signs of distress
> in their communities that might threaten their
> households. When enviromental "accidents"
> occur, it is these women who are typically the first
> to detect a problem. Moreover, because of
> women's unique role in the biological
> regeneration of the species, our bodies are
> important markers, the sites upon which local,
> regional, or even planetary stress is often played
> out.[3]

Community life, as we have seen, has been eviscerated by the
market, largely replaced by "an all-encompassing, wildly deper-
sonalizing bureaucracy," as Bookchin puts it: "The agency and the
bureaucrat have become the substitutes for the family, the town and
neighborhood."[4] In the face of the massive bureaucratization and
commodification of life, ecofeminists—like most radical ecologists—believe that we can build ecological societies at the commu-

nity level, where people can meet and interact with each other on a face-to-face basis, care for each other, and know each other. Social ecologists, long before ecofeminists, argued that the preservation and reconstruction of community life is necessary for an ecological society. Insofar as community life has been eviscerated in European and American cultures, ecology movements there seek in various ways to preserve and restore community life as essential to the ethical fabric of human existence.

Indeed, it is here that the ecology and ecofeminist movements share aspirations with movements to oppose development in Third World countries. In non-Western cultures, many people seek to protect not only their natural environments but their very cultures and communities against the toxicity of Western development. Women in Third World cultures, as Diamond and Orenstein note, have spoken out strongly against the spread of these toxicities:

> In many ways, women's struggle in the rural Third World is of necessity also an ecological struggle. Because so many women's lives are intimately involved in trying to sustain and conserve water, land, and forests, they understand in an immediate way the contrasts of technologies that pillage the Earth's natural riches.[5]

To be sure, women have been much involved in ecological struggles, in both industrialized and Third World cultures, sometimes at the forefront, sometimes not—few would argue that Chico Mendes, the martyred organizer of rubber tappers in the Brazilian rainforest, was a woman. Moreover, whether all women involved in ecological struggles would call themselves ecofeminists is another question entirely. At least one American feminist environmental activist considers ecofeminist writings to be "hopelessly abstract, gorged on rhetoric, humorless, full of resentment toward professionals and achievement, and above all, tiresome." Author Anne Cameron considers the term *ecofeminist* to be an "insult" to feminist activists—ironically, in an article in an anthology subtitled *The Promise of Ecofeminism.*[6]

In any case, "community" and the communitarian ethos have been controversial subjects of discussion in radical political thought in recent years. Some theorists have rightly pointed out, for example, that life in previous communitarian contexts has been notoriously oppressive to women. We cannot ignore the fact that male-oriented cosmologies have invoked "nature" pure and simple as a prescriptive ethical order for society and disdainfully defined women by their biological role in reproduction. Clearly, any serious attempt to work with the concept of community must grapple with this patricentric tradition of women's "naturally" prescribed inferiority.

Moreover, the decentralized community, seen abstractly without due regard to democracy and confederalism, has the potential to become regressive in other ways as well. Homophobia, anti-Semitism, and racism, as well as sexism, may become part of a parochial "communitarian" ethos that does not confront the troubling history of "naturalistic" prescriptions of "inferiority" or "perversion" that are applied to certain groups of people. Thus, the communitarian ethos has a history of repressiveness and parochialism that cannot be ignored.

Given this history of community, then, it is necessary for the ecology movement generally to carefully rethink how it is going to construct community in a liberatory sense, so that such problems can be avoided. The new communities that we construct must not contain the hierarchical features, for example, of the communities that capitalism destroyed. It is necessary to understand what an enlightened community should be, one that preserves the closeness and intimacy and camaraderie of community life, yet that would not be so parochial as to permit black men and women once again to be excluded or white women and women of color to be raped or deprived of their reproductive freedom.

The only way that community can be restored in a liberatory way is if there is some way that people can make general decisions about the life of the community as a whole. If we are going to have community life that is liberatory for women, the community must have an arena where *all* of its members can democratically decide such basic questions. We cannot have liberatory communities

today without the Enlightenment's legacy emphasizing the importance of the individual—however much the Enlightenment dis-
torted that individual into a self-interested ego (without the right
to political dissent, or without the combined Greek and Enlightenment legacy of democratic decision-making).

Although the Greek word *oikos* originally did mean "household," we must recall that the household alone did not make up
the Greek community any more than the *polis* alone did. The Greek
community was formed by the melding of the *polis* with the *oikos,*
in which the former rested on the latter, however much it disdained
it. Thus, ecofeminists cannot slip so casually from "*oikos*" to
"community." Any community must have a public realm—where
general matters are considered—as well as a more intimate realm
of childrearing and familial relationships. Thus, ecofeminist Cynthia Hamilton is quite right to call for "direct participatory democracy."[7] Without this general realm of direct participatory
democracy, community life runs the risk of becoming as oppressive
as it once was, even if it is also intimate and integrated with the
fabric of the natural world.

But for the most part, aside from lonely voices like Hamilton's,
ecofeminist writings are remarkably bereft of references to democracy. The most common approach is simply to ignore the question
of the *polis* altogether and concentrate on the presumed "women's
values" of the *oikos.* Thus, while these writings are filled with
discussions of "oneness," "aliveness," "goddesses," and "interconnectedness," they provide very little vision of the democratic
processes that can keep these new "ecological" values from transforming communities into tyrannies, the way they have developed
historically (as we have seen), or keep community life from deteri-
orating into oppressive parochialisms, as has also been the case
historically. Clearly established, distinct face-to-face democratic
institutions, as specifically human "forms of freedom" (to use
Bookchin's phrase), are essential to a liberatory—rather than a
repressive—community.

Some ecofeminists who refer to the ideas of democratic politics actually do so in a pejorative way. Ynestra King sees the
democratic political tradition as historically contrary to organic

community. "The Western male bourgeois...extracts himself from the realm of the organic to become a public citizen, as if born from the head of Zeus"—as if the words "public citizen" denote nothing but the grasping "male bourgeois" ego concerned only with self-interest! For King, to draw on "the Western democratic tradition" is to "work...with a political legacy that is founded on the repudiation of the organic, the female, the tribal, and particular ties between people...I am mindful that the original citizen in that tradition is male, propertied, and xenophobic."[8] This is convoluted thinking and atavism with a vengeance, especially if one considers that the Western democratic tradition produced a consciousness of *universal* freedom that ultimately opened the public sphere to women and advanced beyond the parochialism of "tribal" life with its focus on the blood tie.

As most people in European and American culture learn early in their school years, in an *ideal* democratic decision-making process, differing views on a given issue are argued out publicly. After everyone has heard all sides, they take a vote. The view that gains the majority of votes passes. Since politics in this ideal sense concerns itself with the affairs of the general community, and since any community will contain people with varying personal views, majority rule has long been seen as the most democratic way to make decisions. While the decision of the majority passes, those who hold the minority view have the right to dissent until they can persuade the majority. The decision of the majority may well be the wrong decision initially and may even by challenged by civil disobedience, if opponents of a decision are prepared to face the consequences of their actions, in an *authentic* democracy. But the ideal democratic process allows those who disagree at the time to argue their position and *remain publicly dissociated* from what they consider the wrong decision. This admittedly is a far from perfect solution, but at least it is explicit. Minorities are not coerced to obey the decision of a majority; rather, the differences are open, clear, and definable. In an authentic democracy, we can reasonably expect that experience will eventually provide evidence of whether a majority's decision is correct or not, as long as the democratic process is an open one and allows for change in repeated gatherings of the community to evaluate its decisions and revoke them where they are evidently wrong.

By contrast, many ecofeminists prefer consensus decision-making to that of majority-minority democracy. Ideally, consensus process seeks group unanimity. In the ideal consensus process, no decision is made by a group without unanimity. After a period of debate on an issue, according to consensus theorist Caroline Estes, "there starts to emerge a common answer to the question that moves the group to a decision." This is a prayer at best rather than a description, for sometimes a "common answer" does not emerge at all. Ideal consensus and consensus-seeking processes are nonetheless premised on the notion that such a "common answer" must *always* emerge if a decision is to be made, not unlike the emphasis many ecofeminists place on the "oneness" of "all" in a cosmological sense. Says Estes, "It is fairly easy to arrive at a unity place where people can get behind and move forward together." Indeed, for Estes, consensus is a matter of urgency: "This integration is going to be essential for our survival."[9]

By affirming that this "integration" is "essential for our survival," Estes creates a quasi-authoritarian imperative. We are left with the impression that there must be "unity"—or else! Estes' affirmation of group unity thus conceals the fact that she dispenses with the notions of majority rule and minority dissent so basic to the ultimate recourse of all democratic decision-making. Estes, rather, argues that "we can no longer have majorities and minorities: we need collective unity." She calls the consensus process "a feminine form of decision-making: it is unifying, it is sharing, it is caring, it is nondominant, it is empowering." Although she regards her vision of consensus as "nondominant," Estes also describes a collective "wisdom" that individuals may well be cautious about challenging:

> It's very rare that any of us has the audacity to think that we have more wisdom than the collective wisdom of the group. And when those occasions occur, it is very difficult for us to take that stand. You must be terribly sure.[10]

Such imperatives and commandments have a very chilling ring to them. The fate of individual dissent in consensus as Estes describes it involves its elimination—and this today, at a time when dissent itself is already in tatters. What is important in the ecological concept of "unity in diversity" is the recognition that diversity can exist without destroying the unity of a community. In Estes' formulations, diversity—let alone dissent—is literally erased through the moral coercion of consensus-seeking by "unity." (The problem is not resolved by such gimmicks as having dissenters "step out" of the decision-making process, as Estes proposes, which simply obliges dissenters to step out of the political process altogether.) "Unity" and "integration" are given almost metaphyiscal, if not quasi-religious, qualities that smother personal independence and disagreement. One can only applaud people like Johann Weyer and Reginald Scot, who did not have Estes' high opinion of "group wisdom." These brave 16th-century writers courageously stood up to the "collective wisdom" of their day that was insanely persecuting and burning women as witches. Recent attempts to impose consensus on "collectivities" have often led to grim results. In 1978, for example, the Clamshell Alliance, a vibrant anti-nuclear group in New England, was nearly destroyed when some of its more media-hungry members used the tyranny of "moral persuasion" to attain consensus on turning a militant occupation of the Seabrook reactor into a vapid theatrical event.

Consensus is a form of decision-making most appropriate for small, intimate groups—for families and friends. It presupposes a certain commonality of views that emerge from shared experiences and affinities. But we encounter problems in larger, more heterogeneous, public spheres, where conflicts of opinion are not only inevitable but even desirable. Benign as consensus may seem to some at first glance, its seeming "organicity" in the past stemmed largely from the power of entrenched custom and the pressure of public opinion in tribal societies and certain religious groups, not merely "collective wisdom." Today, total agreement on issues can easily reflect a degree of homogenization or demands for conformity that stunt personal and social creativity. Dissent is not merely a form of disagreement. It is a form of healthy and creative *opposi-*

tion that gives rise to new ideas and critical thinking. To disparage dissent as "the audacity to think that we have more wisdom than the collective wisdom of the group" is to foster passivity, compliance, and even fear to voice one's opinions, to subordinate the individual to the group, to force the idiosyncratic and the original to adapt to the conventional, and to reduce creativity of thought to the lowest common denominator. No view is less democratic, in reality, than one that homogenizes everyone on the basis of the mystical principle of the "feminine," which as we have seen has a fearful eternality of its own. For an ecofeminist like Helen Forsey "the issue of tolerance is a thorny one. How much are we willing to tolerate actions and attitudes that go against our cherished values?"[11] Forsey herself does not answer her own question, and indeed, it is one that ecofeminists—redefining community as *oikos*—must openly confront.

But the many brief essays by the variety of writers that make up ecofeminist "theory" rarely manage to answer this crucial question, or even raise the question of democracy itself. The numerous ecofeminists who ignore the subject of democracy altogether seem to feel that "women's values" of "caring and nurturing" constitute a compassionate and organic alternative to the presumably cold, abstract, individualistic, and rationalistic—if not outright "masculine" or "male"—democratic ideal. The ethos of motherhood is a "paradigm" for ecofeminist Arisika Razak, for example, since "birth is *the* primary numinous event." Indeed, for Razak,

> Birth is such a universal and central aspect of human existence that it can serve as the nucleus around which to build a paradigm for positive human interaction.... If we begin with loving care for the young, and extend that to social caring for *all* people and personal concern for the planet, we would have a different world. If we understood and celebrated birth, we'd...reclaim the importance of love and warmth and genuine human interaction. (emphasis added)[12]

Presumably, we can attain our ecological ideal of a more humane and sharing community if we revalue the ethos of the domestic realm, of the *oikos,* instead of committing ourselves to the seemingly impersonal *polis.* Apparently, the ethos of the *oikos* can somehow transcend even the need for a *polis,* as if valuing "caring and nurturing" render a political arena unnecessary, dissolve dissent as merely illusory and artificial in the light of "the primary numinous event." Presumably, if we "remember" our dependency on women who gave us birth (a rather self-serving, if not chauvinistic, notion that excludes males), we will understand that disagreements are illusions that "divide" us. Presumably, if the *oikos* makes up the community, political life is unnecessary.

That ecofeminists make allusions to the Western democratic tradition often in a derogatory fashion is very disquieting. Given the massive bureacratization of what passes for "political life" today—the nation-state—it is understandable that ecofeminists might call for a more personal, "caring" approach to community life. The call for a caring approach is one with which few radical ecologists—and certainly not social ecologists—would disagree.

But their glorification of the *oikos* and its values as a substitute for the *polis* and its politics can easily be read as an attempt to dissolve the political into the domestic, the civil into the familial, the public into the private. Just as certain bureaucratic state institutions seem to loom over us, casting a shadow over our freedom, so there is the danger that the *oikos* will loom over us, casting a shadow over our autonomy. The *oikos,* or home, is by no means the magic talisman that will provide the framework for a caring world. Not only is it often narrow-minded, self-enclosed, and incestuous; it can also produce—as it has in history—the very opposite sentiments from those that ecofeminists prize. Indeed the *oikos* has not only been women's realm, but *also men's.* It has provided a home not only for male hunters, food-gatherers, and farmers, but also warriors, kings, and patriarchal tyrants.

To mystify the *oikos* and ignore or criticize the Western democratic tradition raises the strong possibility that ecofeminists will ignore some of the ugly social traits the *oikos* has produced historically. Other feminists have long understood that the *oikos* was the world of entrapment, of home economics, from which they fought bitterly and valiantly to escape, indeed, the locus classicus of patriarchy, as in the Greek *oikos* itself. They sought a larger world than childrearing, food-preparing, and connubial "bliss." In short, they wanted to become full participants in society—*citizens*—not remain domesticated drones. Perhaps one of the most regressive features of ecofeminism generally is that even as it condemns patriarchy, it seeks to return society to the *oikos* in a way that ignores its oppressive and suffocating dimensions, and how easily men made the *oikos* their own sovereign domain.

Public and Private in History

Doubtless, there once was a time when society consisted of only an *oikos,* with no *polis.* In hunting-gathering and foraging cultures that survive today and presumably existed in ancient cultures, the public and private domains are hardly distinguished at all. The cultures of the early Neolithic in Eastern Europe, for example, were most likely domestic societies that had no distinct public realm. Tribal societies are organized not according to any concept of a general humanity, for example, but according to family ties, or the blood tie. Unlike the atomized, grasping "individual" today, in tribal societies individuals are deeply integrated into the kinship system and traditional local social relationships.

Doubtless, too, it is true that life in societies organized around kinship was more benign than life in our own society in many personal ways. Kinship societies were small in scale and fostered a degree of intimacy that other societies often lack. They recognized the interdependency of all individuals within the group and they enjoyed a morality based on reciprocity, with clearly fixed obligations and duties, so that everyone was cared for in the basic needs of life. Everyone also had a clearly defined role and knew what he or she was obliged to do and what others were obliged to do in return. Land was often "owned" in common, and people used only what they needed of the common resources of the community. Such

positive aspects of tribal society could well serve to enhance and
enrich the democratic political tradition.

Finally, since the family realm in tribal organic societies
formed the authentic core of social life, the fact that women played
a central role in the domestic realm tended to give them considerable status. Anthropologist Michelle Z. Rosaldo once noted that the
cultures in which gender is most "egalitarian" are "those in which
public and domestic spheres are only weakly differentiated, where
neither sex claims much authority and the force of social life itself
is the home."[13] Early matrilineal societies seem in fact to have been
quite egalitarian, and women's participation was likely of central
importance, as we have seen in Chapter 2.

But we should not ignore the warts in early organic kinship
society, ones that would make Western and other peoples today
very uncomfortable. The past has a great deal to teach us, but we
should not embrace it uncritically. Perhaps the most serious problem that organic tribal society faced in the past was the fact that it
was organized according to the blood tie, or a shared tie imputed
to a common ancestor. The blood tie was overarching as a way of
describing one's loyalties. Unchangeable in theory, at least, it froze
social organization into patterns set by birth, age, and sex. People
had no control over the seemingly biological factors that often
determined their social position. In this sense, these kinship societies were not moral, strictly speaking, because social roles were
limited by a commitment to biological attributes, not to rational
ones. Like it or not, one owed one's loyalties to a biologically
constitued form of association that tended to narrow one's sense of
belonging to a larger social order.

Moreover, since political groupings, in effect, were the same
as family groupings, membership in a political group often depended on being born into it. That is, kinship tended to be exclusive. The "good life" in a tribe or clan usually remained the
privilege of the person born to it. Because it was based on a real or
putative blood tie, the "moral" obligations of kinship life often did
not extend beyond the kin group: "The community based on
association through kinship alone, finds it impossible to recognize
itself in other communities that do not share common ancestral

lineages."[14] Those outside the kinship group were not entitled to the protection of the community. Codes of hospitality toward visitors were variable. Non-kin people had no guaranteed rights and status in relation to the kin group and could even be regarded as enemies. As Bookchin writes,

> Aside from its lavish code of hospitality, organic society made no real provision for the rights of the stranger, the outsider, who was not linked by marriage or ritual to the kin group. The larger world beyond the perimeter of "The People" was "inorganic." Loyalties extended in varying degrees of obligation to those who shared the common blood oath of the community and to allies united by material systems of gift reciprocity. The notion of a humanity in which all human beings are considered united by a common genesis was still largely alien.[15]

Because of the virtual exclusivity of early kinship systems, then, they did not adequately solve the problem of how to deal with people who were not kin, except by marriage alliances, adoption, and other extensions of the shared ancestry to the point of fiction. Human political and social existence remained parochial and particularized into family groups. Unless humanity was to remain completely isolated in small exclusive communities, early organic societies had to find some way of establishing suprablood relations so that non-kin individuals could interact with each other without incurring blood feuds.

That is, it was necessary, sooner or later, to create a public sphere in which "the stranger"—the non-kin individual—could be a community member on the basis of a shared humanity, not birth. It was for this reason that the public realm slowly emerged out of the private *oikos,* especially in the West. In the emerging public realm, strangers could begin to find a place in the community. They could be dealt with amicably, as resident aliens or as citizens, or they could be dealt with hostilely, as in warfare, but they could be dealt with—by increasingly rational rather than customary patterns of behavior. But ultimately, in early organic societies, the domestic realm was the women's realm, and the emerging public realm was the men's realm, a configuration that has persisted in the West for millennia since. But in its beginnings, the public realm did not necessarily exist in a hierarchical relationship with the domestic. It may well be an instance of present-day hierarchical thinking that we see the public and domestic in hierarchical terms. In fact, the public and domestic realms probably coexisted on equal terms for a long period of time before the public realm gradually gained ascendance over the domestic. The two were initially complementary to each other.

Needless to say, the public realm not only gained ascendance, it developed extremely hierarchal structures of its own. Through various combinations of emerging stratification, force, and also invasion, through a history of greater and lesser degrees of what Bookchin calls "statification," the public realm developed from warrior elites into the extraordinarily hierarchial one with which we are familiar today and from the past. And indeed, during times when the public realm was less powerful and the *oikos* had prominence once again—as in the 9th and 10th centuries A.D.—European women exercised a relatively prominent role in social affairs.[16]

But in the light of this history, to glorify women's domestic realm as "caring" and "nurturing" without emphasizing how easily it could be manipulated by men or, worse, become a refuge for the weary warrior, is to mystify the relationship of the domestic to the public—presumably "women's world" to that of men. For although kinship societies look after their own and may therefore be said to be caring, nothing in the kinship ethos—or in the domestic, for that matter—prevents stratification from emerging out of biologically delineated ranking systems like age, gender, and blood ties. Not even the Neolithic "ethic of care" could prevent this development (which is perhaps why "Kurgan invasions" are such a convenient ploy for many ecofeminists). Indeed, paradoxically, "caring" is remarkably compatible with hierarchy. An ethic of motherly care thus does not *by itself* pose a threat to hierarchy and domination.

The emergence of the patriarchal family—in which the father, not the mother ruled—was a development that occurred precisely within the domestic realm. In ancient Athens, of course, it was the father, not the mother, who ruled in the *oikos.* Perhaps the earliest slaves were women "weavers" and servants whom patriarchs brought to the service of their wives and families. Indeed, the biological rankings of organic tribal society were themselves ultimately used as rationales for increasing stratification and power, such as in many societies in the ancient world. Egypt, for example, was not a "political" state in the sense we know it today—it was an oversized, aggrandized *oikos.* The very word "pharaoh" means "great house," and in his "great house," the fixed status rankings of hierarchical tribal society were not only retained but exacerbated, and mystified into a theocracy to boot. Moreover, as wealth was accumulated in early societies generally, it was kept in the domestic *oikos* by virtue of being transmitted through kinship lines. It was the blood tie that underpinned and continues to underpin aristocratic lineages—keeping wealth in the domestic realm of privileged families.

The *oikos,* as it evolved through history, has thus not been "women's realm" alone. Perhaps most compellingly for our discussion, the private *oikos* encompasses not only the *domestic* realm but also the *economic* realm, the realm of private interests. *Oikos* is, after all, the root not only of the word "ecology" but also of the word "economics." Indeed, the interests of early capitalists were quintessentially *private* interests. Early capitalists justified the unequal distribution of wealth that they caused by invoking what they saw as their private deserts, their personal abilities, their entrepreneurial savvy—and very often, their family traditions, to the point of absurd nepotism. All of the important capitalists of the 19th century and well into the 20th were known by their family names—such as the Astors, the Rockefellers, the Morgans, and the Krupps.

Thus, the word *oikos* has at least a double meaning. It can mean home—the domestic realm—to be sure, as ecofeminists argue; it can also mean economy. It was the "*oikos*" of the private interests of capital that unleashed enormous productive forces and that is now used to wreak such havoc on the biosphere and on community life. Ironically, the "*oikos*" of economics is now destroying the "*oikos*" of ecology.

The Public Realm

If the *private realm* has varying senses—ranging from the "household" to the family fortunes of capitalists—so does the *public realm* have a double meaning: "the state" and "the democratic polity." The operations of the state in the public realm have produced the huge centralized bureaucracies that dehumanize people and protect the private interests of capital, to which we are accustomed today. But although today we normally think of the public realm as exclusively the state, the state is only one kind of public realm. In addition, there is another kind of public realm that can legitimately be called *politics* in the original Greek democratic sense of managing the *polis*. Indeed, it was this political realm that emerged, particularly in Athens, to *challenge* the interests of privilege and status, not to *protect* them. Despite the limitations that seriously tainted it—its patriarchy, its slavery—the Athenian democratic *polis* developed as a relatively egalitarian response to many of the hierarchies of both the public and private realms that had developed before it.

The democratic *polis* emerged in part as a response to hierarchy in the public realm—the warrior class of its aristocrats. The Athenian democrats established the ideal—however much it was honored in the breach—of resolving internecine conflicts not through mutual slaughter, but through reasoned argumentation—in contrast to despotic or oligarchic rule. When a citizen argued a position, his aim was to persuade his opponents, not to use violence against them, as had been done earlier in Greek history. Hence the enormous emphasis on discourse and reason, which provided the initiating impulse for much of Greek philosophy. That the citizens of the *polis* tried to resolve disputes through rhetorical conflicts of ideas rather than turn to violence was a radical advance in human affairs, however much this ideal was not always realized. To use one of Bookchin's formulations: "In the Greek mind, where discourse ended, fighting began; hence the importance of rational discussion in Athens."[17]

The Athenian *polis* also defined itself in contrast to Near Eastern societies, which it regarded as despotic rather than rational. Its fears of despotism, moreover, were well founded. Once the *polis* was established, the primary effort of the citizen was directed against threats that were external to the *polis*—notably, attacks by "barbarians" (who included everyone but Greeks)—that would have undermined the community as a unique living organism. Thus, never did Athens rest secure, nor was it ever at peace with all its neighbors.

The Athenian democratic *polis* developed not only to challenge the hierarchies of the public realm, but to contest the hierarchy and exclusivity of kinship society: the increasingly stratified aristocratic family interests in its immediate past. Exclusivity had been a problem because membership in particular kin groups—clans—was a prerequisite for participation in public affairs of general concern. But such membership could be obtained only by birth. Moreover, wealth was becoming increasingly concentrated in certain clans. The clans' control of religion was yet another stratification that caused bitterness; certain clans had become the priestly caste, controlling the religious life of the general population.

The Athenian democracy tried to break down this private stratification and exclusivity. By the end of the sixth century B.C.E. Kleisthenes took the remarkable step of abolishing the blood tie altogether as the basis for political organization and thereby destroyed the political power of privileged clans. This ended kin exclusivity as a criterion for political participation. By dividing people geographically instead of according to blood constituencies, Kleisthenes abolished the power of tribal and kinship ties. Residence eventually became the basis for citizenship in the *polis,* albeit only of Athenian men.

For classical Greek political philosophers, the *oikos* on which the citizen body rested and depended was the realm of the particular, whereas the *polis* was, relatively speaking, the realm of the universal, of public legislation and fair trials by peers. The political realm—occupied by men—was seen as having a more universalistic orientation than the *oikos,* concerned with the management of the community as a whole. The Athenian democratic *polis* now regarded private interests as particularistic, not only those of wealthy aristocrats but the claims of the domestic *oikos* itself.

Obviously, the Athenian democratic *polis* did not contest the hierarchy in its own *oikoi,* and thereby did not actualize the potentiality of its own innovation. And it excluded people from citizenship—not only women, but slaves, male Greeks from other poleis, and resident aliens. But what the Athenians regarded as universal, as transcending kin among all peoples, were the same attributes that they believed made citizens politically equal: the human capacity for rationality. It must be emphasized that the *potentiality* for including everyone in citizenship was present in the democratic framework that the Athenians devised, even if it was not fulfilled.

This potentiality does not exist in kinship groups. Although kinship organization and *polis* organization were both exclusive in their own ways, the kinship system, however contrived, could not be broadened without violating its very essence—the idea of the blood tie and shared ancestry. Kinship organization was exclusive by definition. The biological accidents of birth and of common ancestry—however fictitious they were in many communities—ultimately decided membership in the community.

Nor is the emotion of "caring" something that one can authentically extend to "all people," as Razak puts it. Even the human beings who are most caring cannot extend caring to *everyone.* As an emotion, "caring" cannot be universalized as the basis for social organization outside one's own small group, whether kinship-based or not. Nor can the kind of caring that a mother (or father) feels for a child be universalized—irrespective of whether one "thinks like a mountain" or "allows oneself to be a tree." People can certainly achieve a universal recognition of their shared humanity—witness our concerns for the fate of people who suffer disasters in every part of the world. But they can hardly know every human being in the world or care intimately for all unknown individuals in the same sense that a mother cares intimately for a child or members of her family. To propose to care for "all people" would be to make the concept of "caring" so broad as to be meaningless and unfocused.

Nor is "caring" in itself anti-hierarchical, any more than kinship organization was. The "mothering" ideal itself is not inherently democratic, as Mary Dietz has pointed out, nor does it necessarily foster freedom. "There is no reason to think that mothering necessarily induces commitment to democratic practices," she observes,

> nor are there good grounds for arguing that a principle like "care for vulnerable human life"...by definition encompasses a defense of participatory citizenship. An enlightened despotism, a welfare state, a single-party bureaucracy, and a democratic republic may all respect mothers, protect children's lives, and show compassion for the vulnerable.[18]

Not only is "caring" compatible with hierarchy, if it is in any way grounded in "women's nature"—or men's for that matter—but it lacks any institutional form. It simply rests on the tenuous prayer that individuals will be motivated to "care." But individuals may easily start or stop caring. They may care at their whim. They may not care enough. They may care about some but not others. Lacking an institutional form and dependent on individual whim, "caring" is a slender thread on which to base an emancipatory political life.

But if kinship and caring are by their very nature particular and limited, democratic politics is expandable and potentially all-inclusive. The essence of democracy is precisely its latent capacity to cut across particular ethnic, gender, and other cultural lines. The Athenian impulse to "universalize"—as limited as it was in its time—came from a recognition of a humanity that went beyond the exclusivity of the blood tie. And as the definition of citizenship was extended historically—initially by the Emperor Caracalla—the rights, privileges, and responsibilities of political life were extended as well.

Creating a New Political Realm

Social ecology distinguishes between statecraft, as a system of dealing with the public realm by means of professionalized administrators and their legal monopoly on violence, on the one hand, and politics, as the management of the community on a grassroots democratic and face-to-face level by citizen bodies, on the other. The libertarian municipalism of social ecology provides a framework for recreating political life as a participatory democratic process.[19] Thus, the political sphere is not only preserved and widely expanded, but the concept of politics is reformulated to bring decision-making as close to the people as possible—that is, to the most grassroots level that is politically attainable, such as popular assemblies.

The struggle to contest the private interests that are destroying the biosphere must be a political struggle. It must be organized around the creation of this new oppositional political realm of face-to-face participatory democracy. Indeed, the importance of a vital public realm for ecological politics is incalculable. Nothing less than the elimination of capitalism and the nation-state—indeed, the restructuring of society into decentralized, cooperative communities—will make a healthy, concerned public *and* private life possible. The democratic political realm—as opposed to the statist public realm—is the only realm we have that has the potential to contest both the private interests that are destroying the biosphere and the public hierarchies that attempt to degrade and instrumentalize human beings. Even as ecofeminists seem to be writing the *polis* out of their community in favor of the *oikos,* they are eliminating the one arena that can seriously challenge hierarchy in both the public and private realms: participatory democratic politics.

The libertarian municipalist approach of social ecology advocates local solutions wherever they are possible. Decentralized social arrangements would make it possible to assure that all individuals, male and female, have complete access to political life.

In this new political realm, any conflicting private interests that exist within a community can be confronted and argued in full view of every citizen. This polity is held together not by religion but by a common political ideal and an educated citizenry, whose very raison d'être is discussion and debate, argumentation and agreement, clashes of ideas and concerns, and decision-making by the majority—needless to say, with minorities free to publicly dissent. As part of the community, a local face-to-face democratic polity would be embedded in the mutual interdependency of its citizens. To the extent that both women and men come into their fullness as public and private participants, they infuse political life with concern as well as affection for those with whom they have worked so hard, and those with whom they are avowedly interdependent.

As municipal democratic political arenas are expanded and strengthened by popular participation, they can join together to constitute a dual power to the authority of the state. This dual power would be strong because it emanates from popular institutions, institutions in which citizens maintain their democratic freedoms. Thus we would see the embodiment of the communitarian ideal in a new, enlightened form.

Clearly, the interests of capital transcend even the boundaries of the nation-state, let alone those of the community. Fighting large economic entities that operate even on the international level requires large numbers of municipalities to work together. To address macrosocial forces like capitalism, the political communities, according to a libertarian municipalist approach, would restore the principle of *confederation*—a principle that for centuries has been advanced by radical thinkers as an alternative to the nation-state. Lest we forget this great historic tradition and its clash with statecraft, confederation is the grassroots linkage of communities on neighborhood, citywide, district, county, and regional levels in such a way that power flows from the bottom up rather than from the top down as it does in the nation-state. In a confederal society, the "higher" we go in coordinating our efforts to administer society, the more the right to formulate policy becomes diminished, until the "highest" confederal councils have no power but those of coordination and administration. The formulation of *policy,* in short, is made at the grassroots level of society, and its *administration* is executed by confederal councils. Needless to say, in a truly democratic polity, people are free to argue their individual views in a face-to-face manner, not assign their rights to representatives who may or may not be subject to the pressures of particularistic interests. Policy decisions are made by the people, not by representatives.

As such, democratic citizenship in the political realm has its own distinct virtues, its own distinct ways of behaving, its own distinct relations, as Mary Dietz has pointed out. "Its relation is that of civic peers; its guiding virtue is mutual respect; its primary principle is the 'positive liberty' of democracy and self-government, not simply the 'negative liberty' of noninterference."[20] Insofar as citizens in a democratic polity are engaged in dealing with issues of public concern, they would find it very difficult to allow their private interests to deflect them. At the very least, one's attention would be directed outward, not only inward to purely spiritual or intimate concerns. Democratic process involves the acceptance of objective, external political procedures, which can mean the deferral or postponement of private, particularistic interests that are not supportive of the public welfare as a whole.

Let me make it quite clear that I do not contend that personal life must be sacrificed to political life. Quite to the contrary, I believe that the two of them have to coexist in a balanced, rational, and truly ecological manner. Attention to the personal in itself is and always will be of great individual as well as social concern. Human beings have vital needs for self-expression, love, play, a relationship with a particular place, with nonhuman nature, as well as intimate relationships with other people. They have a vital need for a spiritual dimension in their lives—in the broadest sense of the word "spiritual"—a dimension that is sorely lacking in our society. All of these needs have strong social implications and cannot be isolated from the kinds of institutions, communities, and forms of association we should establish in an ecological society.

But we must also recognize that certain distinctions do exist between the personal and the political in this sense. The intimacies that we develop in personal life cannot be carried over *wholesale* into the relations we must establish in a democratic politics. Not everyone can know everyone who makes up a sizeable community—certainly not to the extent that one knows the members of one's family, one's lovers, one's personal friends, and other intimates. It should be clear that a certain amount of objectivity is necessary for conducting political affairs that involve individuals who are not one's intimates. Beyond the circle of one's intimates, political institutions must be established that involve the participation of sizeable numbers of people, especially if we seek to attain a participatory democracy. The precondition for such a democracy is the delicately formed institutional fabric through which dissent as well as agreement can be adequately expressed. In short, there must be organized and coordinated structures that make both political and personal freedom possible.

In any democratic polity worthy of the name, one is accountable to one's fellow citizens, not only to one's friends and lovers. Even in the political life of a local community, a certain amount of objectivity is unavoidable—for example, to assure that everyone is free to exercise her or his rights, or that decisions have been properly carried out, or that no favoritism has been shown, or that minorities may freely dissent. A certain objective framework must be established in order that the interplay of conflicting views can be expressed in a creative and educational manner. Citizens cannot be expected to learn of others' views or answer challenges to their own if their differences are muted by a moral tyranny of consensus-seeking or by the growing belief that all ideological conflicts are forms of violence. Even if one were to adopt a consensus process of decision-making, one would at least require an objective facilitator. This objectivity is not a matter of alienation or an absence of concern or caring, nor is it a matter of "controlling and regulating nature," to use Plant's formulation.[21] It is merely a matter of behaving in a mature, responsible, and fair-minded manner in which everyone has the opportunity to fully express her or his ideas.

The virtues, relations, and practices that are necessary for a participatory democracy are not "male" or "masculine" ones but _human_ ones. As political creatures, human beings as such can manage the affairs of the community so that individuals within it can fulfill themselves. Political movements depend on the willingness of clear-thinking, critical, individuated citizens to fight for principles—sometimes above and beyond their personal needs. Instead of working to replace the virtues of the *polis* with those of an *oikos* that has historically oppressed them, women in ecological movements must become involved in the political world as part of a truly liberatory politics and claim citizenship for themselves. They must at long last break out of the *oikos*—whether that is the literal *oikos* of the household or the figurative *oikos* of "women's values"—and work to expand the full range of their *human* capacities. This does not mean that women cease to be women, with the full recognition of their own uniqueness and qualities, but that they transcend the suffocating restrictions that have been long placed on the development of their capacities as people by patricentric society.

Their human capacities—including the capacity to reason—are quite equal to those of men. Women's biology is not simply a matter of reproductive organs—it is a matter of their minds and the intellectual capacities those minds provide. Their minds are part of their human nature, and make them fully capable of rational thought and of political participation, as well as a wealth of other sensibilities. Moral and political agency on the part of both women and men gives them the revolutionary potential to challenge not only "biology as destiny" but also whatever oppressive social constructions and sociopolitical structures they encounter. Admitting "woman = nature" social constructions that enforce patricentricity into a movement that calls itself feminist is a Trojan horse. For an ecological feminism to be liberatory for women, it must be committed to expanding the range of their choices against deterministic forces, whether biological, cultural, or economic, not to the narrowing of politics to an "intimate private" domain. If women in ecology movements are to "find their way," it must be a way that brings them out of the *oikos,* not one that thrusts them back into it in the name of a domestic ethos of "caring," "nurturing," and the evocation of a cryptic and mystical "biologism" in the name of organic or tribal ties.

History clearly belies any assertion that women are congenitally unsuited for political life, or that the Western democratic ideal is hopelessly compromised by its emergence from a sexist culture. Indeed, the very logic of democracy demands the inclusion of women, that any counterposition of a "female" *oikos* to a "male" *polis* be overcome. Women's crucial and massive involvement in social movements, in grassroots political work, and in revolutions—such as the French Revolution and the Paris Commune of 1871—has long expanded the circle of their inclusion in the political realm. We must treasure these legacies of political revolt and seek to expand them with the full participation not only of women but of people of color and all other formerly excluded groups. Democratic practices and virtues are inherently neither genderbound nor race-bound. Indeed, their very logic calls for a more all-inclusive community of human beings than any we have ever seen in the past, including the Neolithic village. Far from demanding women's subordination, participatory democracy presupposes their inclusion to the full capacity of their beings.

It is unfashionable to speak of "human nature" in the 1990s. The present radical political culture, to the extent that one exists in the 1990s, most often rejects the universal in favor of the particular and parochial. But the fact is that women alone do not make up a community. The very breadth of the ecological crisis is such that it affects everyone, not women alone. Toxic dumps, nuclear power plants and wastes, polluted water and air, toxic substances in households and workplaces threaten the health and well-being of present and future generations of both sexes wherever they live and work. Moreover, the capacities of reason, language, culture, and consociation for choice and decision-making, for ethical and political behavior, as well as for affection and nurture—are all capacities that people have as human beings, whether they are women or men, gay or straight, of African descent, Caucasian, Jewish, Hispanic, Asian, Arab, Native American, or any combination thereof.

Social ecology provides a basis for the recognition of our common humanity by virtue of our shared natural history in the course of biological evolution or first nature. It is the potential of the ecology movement to become a *general* interest that crosses gender lines. What many ecofeminists claim as an interest of particular concern to women is in fact a general interest—with the community as the locus of struggle, incorporating and going beyond the best democratic aspirations of the classical *polis* and the Enlightenment.

The local "forms of freedom" so necessary for an ecological society in which all domination is ended—forms like neighborhood assemblies, town meetings, and confederal forms of association—are increasingly losing ground to centralized state governments. As European and American governments have become increasingly centralized in this century, the vitality of local political life has increasingly dwindled. Base-democratic institutions will have to be fought for if they are going to survive, or be created where they no longer exist. In a time of massive privatization, we cannot permit what remains of the democratic political sphere to be vitiated further by inward-looking privatistic, particularistic, or *oikos*-oriented tendencies. We must reclaim the political tradition of radical democracy and fight to preserve and expand it.

Such a goal would indeed provide the coordinates for a radically new feminist and social ecology movement in which women together with men can find their way out of the morass that threatens to bog down the vast project of ecological and social fulfillment. It is bad enough that we are all less than human today, that the realm of second nature after thousands of years of progress and perversion has reached the cruel impasse that marks the present era. If women have a "calling," it is not the particularistic—even elitist—one that ecofeminists assign to them. Rather, it is the challenge to rise to a generous ecological humanism, so underlying to the principles of social ecology, and to an all-embracing sense of solidarity, not only with nonhuman life, but with the men who form an integral part of humanity as a whole. To heighten specious gender differences—ironically in the name of an ecological ethos— is to taint ecology and the authentic goals of feminism alike.

Here all thinking women stand at a crossroads. Will they mystify the domestic virtues of the *oikos,* emphasize their particularity, defame the most generous traditions of democracy as "male" or "patriarchal," and ultimately degrade whatever progress humanity as a whole has attained in the course of its development? Or will they pursue a more generous approach by joining with others—men no less than women—in a common project of liberation and ecological restoràtion? This common project can never be formulated merely in terms of domestic values, of atavistic mystical retreats to the "tribalistic" virtues of the Neolithic village, or of direct or indirect denigrations of reason, science, and technology as "male" or "patriarchal." In the ecology movement, thinking women must, if only to realize their own human potentialities, either join with thinking men in developing a new politics, rationality, and science—not to speak of those qualities that make us humane as well as human—or they are likely to follow the ecofeminist path toward a narrow parochialism, primitivism, and irrationalism that will ultimately mystify and support the status quo rather than transcend it by achieving a free ecological society.

ENDNOTES

Introduction

1. Biehl, Janet, "What Is Social Ecofeminism?" Green Perspectives 11 (1988), available from Green Program Project, P.O. Box 111, Burlington, Vermont 05402.

Chapter 1
Problems in Ecofeminism

1. Irene Diamond and Gloria Orenstein, "Introduction," in *Reweaving the World: The Emergence of Ecofeminism*, ed. Irene Diamond and Gloria Orenstein (San Francisco: Sierra Club Books, 1990), p. ix.

2. Ynestra King, "Healing the Wounds: Feminism, Ecology, and Nature/Culture Dualism," in *Gender/Body/Knowledge: Feminist Reconstructions of Being and Knowing*, ed. Alison Jaggar and Susan R. Bordo (New Brunswick, N.J.: Rutgers University Press, 1989), p. 123.

3. Susan Griffin, "Curves Along the Road," in *Reweaving the World*, ed. Diamond and Orenstein, p. 95.

4. Audre Lorde criticized Mary Daly for ignoring the heritage of African women in "An Open Letter to Mary Daly" (in *Sister Outsider: Essays and Speeches* (Trumansburg, NY: Crossing Press, 1984), pp. 66-71). The two recent ecofeminist anthologies (*Reweaving the World*, ed. Diamond and Orenstein, and *Healing the Wounds: The Promise of Ecofeminism*, ed. Judith Plant, [Philadelphia: New Society Publishers, 1989]) contain a wide array of

writings by women of color and Third World women, including Paula Gunn Allen, Rachel L. Bagby, Radha Bhatt, Corinne Kumar d' Souza, Gwaganad, Pamela Philipose, Arisika Razak, and Vandana Shiva, among others.

5. Andrée Collard with Joyce Contrucci, *Rape of the Wild: Man's Violence against Animals and the Earth* (Bloomington and Indianapolis: Indiana University Press, 1989), p. 106.

6. Susan Griffin, *Woman and Nature: The Roaring Inside Her* (New York: Harper and Row, 1978), p. 226.

7. Charlene Spretnak, "Toward an Ecofeminist Spirituality," in *Healing the Wounds,* ed. Plant, p. 129.

8. Charlene Spretnak, "Ecofeminism: Our Roots and Flowering," in *Reweaving the World,* ed. Diamond and Orenstein, pp. 5, 6; "Introduction," in Charlene Spretnak, ed., *The Politics of Women's Spirituality: Essays on the Rise of Spiritual Power within the Feminist Movement* (Garden City, N.Y.: Anchor, 1982), p. xvii-xviii.

9. Simone De Beauvoir, *The Second Sex* (New York: Random House, 1968), p. 144.

10.Ynestra King, "Coming of Age with the Greens," *Zeta* (February 1988): 19; Ynestra King, "Healing the Wounds: Feminism, Ecology, and the Nature Culture Dualism," in *Reweaving the World,* ed. Diamond and Orenstein, p. 117. (This "Healing the Wounds" article by King bears almost the same title as the one cited in note 2, but it is somewhat different.) Judith Plant; "Toward a New World: An Introduction," in *Healing the Wounds,* ed. Plant, p. 1.

11. For criticisms of ecofeminism and related cultural feminism, see, for example, Ellen Willis columns in *The Village Voice,* 23 June 1980, p. 28, and 16-22 July 1980, p. 34; Alice Echols, "The New Feminism of Yin and Yang," in *The Powers of Desire,* ed. Ann Snitow, Sharon Thompson, and Christine Stansell (New York: Monthly Review Press, 1983); Joan Cocks, "Wordless Emotions: Some Critical Reflections on Radical Feminism," *Politics and Society* 13 (1984): 27-57; Susan Prentice, "Taking Sides: What's Wrong with Eco-Feminism?" in *Women and Environ-*

ments (Spring 1988): 9-10 (available from Centre for Urban and Community Studies, 455 Spadina Avenue, Toronto, Ontario M5S 2G8); Mary Morse, "Mother Earth Is No Lady: The Perils of Typecasting Nature as Feminine," *Utne Reader* (May/June 1990): 37.

12. Simone De Beauvoir, in Alice Schwarzer, *After the Second Sex: Conversations with Simone de Beauvoir* (New York: Pantheon, 1984), p. 103.

13. Plato, *Timaeus* in *The collected Dialogues of Plato,* ed. Edith Hamilton and Huntington Cairns, Bollingen series (Princeton, NJ: Princeton University Press, 1961), 42b.

14. Marylin Arthur, "From Medusa to Cleopatra: Women in the Ancient World," in *Becoming Visible: Women in European History,* 2d ed., ed. Renate Bridenthal, Claudia Koonz, and Susan Stuard (Boston: Houghton Mifflin, 1987), p. 91.

15. Ynestra King, "The Ecology of Feminism and the Feminism of Ecology," p. 22; Susan Griffin, "Split Culture," in *Healing the Wounds,* ed. Plant, p. 10ff.

16. Ynestra King, in Peggy Luhrs, "Women, Ecology, and Peace: An Interview with Ynestra King," *Vermont Woman* (October 1988): 10; and "Healing the Wounds," in *Feminist Reconstructions,* Jaggar and Bordo, eds., p. 123.

17. Carolyn Merchant, "Ecofeminism and Feminist Theory," in *Reweaving the World,* ed. Diamond and Orenstein, p. 102, 103.

18. Plant, "Toward a New World," p. 3, and "Searching for Common Ground: Ecofeminism and Bioregionalism," in *Reweaving the World,* ed. Diamond and Orenstein, p. 160.

19. Collard, *Rape of the Wild,* pp. 5, 53.

20. Plant, "Toward a New World," p. 5.

21. Carolyn Merchant, *The Death of Nature: Women, Ecology, and the Scientific Revolution* (San Francisco: Harper and Row, 1980, 1983), p. 2.

22. Blumenfeld, Gina, "What Is to Be Undone in the Women's Movement," *Liberation* (February 1975): 11ff. (Reprints of this ar-

ticle are available from Green Program Project, P.O. Box 111, Burlington, Vermont, 05402.)

23. Plant, "Searching for Common Ground," p. 5.

24. Diamond and Orenstein, "Introduction," p. xi; Starhawk, "Power, Authority, and Mystery: Ecofeminism and Earth-based Spirituality," in *Reweaving the World,* ed. Diamond and Orenstein, p. 74; and many others.

25. Plant, "Searching for Common Ground," p. 160.

26. Starhawk, "Power, Authority, and Mystery," p. 73.

27. Spretnak, "Toward an Ecofeminist Spirituality," p. 131.

Chapter 2
The Neolithic Mystique

1. Riane Eisler, "The Gaia Tradition and the Partnership Future: An Ecofeminist Manifesto," in *Reweaving the World,* ed. Diamond and Orenstein, pp. 23, 33-34.

2. See especially the following writings by Marija Gimbutas: "Proto-Indo-European Culture: The Kurgan Culture during the Fifth, Fourth, and Third Millennia B.C.," in *Indo-European and Indo-Europeans,* ed. George Cardona, Henry M. Hoenigswald, and Alfred Senn (Philadelphia: University of Pennsylvania Press, 1970); "The Beginning of the Bronze Age in Europe and the Indo-Europeans: 3500-2500 B.C.," *Journal of Indo-European Studies* 1 (1973): 163-214; "The First Wave of Eurasian Steppe Pastoralists into Copper Age Europe," *Journal of Indo-European Studies* 5 (1977); "The Kurgan Wave #2 (c. 3400-3200 B.C.) into Europe and the Following Transformation of Culture," *Journal of Indo-European Studies* 8 (1980): 273-315; and *The Goddesses and Gods of Old Europe, 7000-3500 B.C.* (Berkeley and Los Angeles: University of California Press, 1982).

3. Spretnak, "Our Roots and Flowering," p. 110; Mara Lynn Keller, "The Eleusinian Mysteries: Ancient Nature Religion of Demeter and Persephone," in *Reweaving the World,* ed. Diamond and Orenstein, p. 51; Starhawk, *Truth or Dare: Encounters with*

Power, Authority and Mystery (San Francisco: Harper and Row, 1988), p. 7.

4. Eisler, "Ecofeminist Manifesto," pp. 23, 34; Spretnak, "Toward an Ecofeminist Spirituality," p. 131.

5. See Murray Bookchin, *The Ecology of Freedom: The Emergence and Dissolution of Hierarchy* (Palo Alto, Calif.: Cheshire Books, 1982; Montreal: Black Rose Books, 1991), pp. 57-61.

6. Eleanor Leacock, "Women in Egalitarian Societies," in *Becoming Visible,* ed. Bridenthal, Koonz, and Stuard, p. 28.

7. Margaret Ehrenberg, *Women in Prehistory* (Norman and London: University of Oklahoma Press, 1989), pp. 95-96, 99.

8. Ibid., pp. 96-97.

9. Sarunas Milisauskas, *European Prehistory* (New York: Academic Press, 1978), pp. 89-91.

10. Marija Gimbutas, "Obre, Yugoslavia: Two Neolithic Sites," *Archaeology* 23 (October 1970): 297; and "Temples of Old Europe," *Archaeology* (November/December 1980).

11. Eisler, "Ecofeminist Manifesto," p. 34.

12. Quoted in Peter Steinfels, "Idyllic Theory of Goddesses Creates Storm," *New York Times,* 13 February 1990, p. B10.

13. Gimbutas, *Goddesses and Gods,* pp. 142, 196.

14. Ehrenberg, *Women in Prehistory,* p. 70.

15. Bookchin, *Ecology of Freedom,* p. 60.

16. Ehrenberg, *Women in Prehistory,* p. 67.

17. Ibid., p. 75.

18. See Pomeroy's debunking of the "archaeological" evidence for the gender-equality of Minoan Crete in her "Selected Bibliography on Women in Classical Antiquity," in *Women in the Ancient World: The Arethusa Papers,* ed. J. Peradotto and J. P. Sullivan (Albany: State University of New York, 1984), pp. 347-54.

19. Rodney Castleden, *The Knossos Labyrinth: A New View of the "Palace of Minos" at Knossos* (London: Routledge, 1990).

20. Ibid, p. 76; on priestesses, see p. 115-20, 125.

21. Peter Warren, "Knossos: New Excavations and Discoveries," *Archaeology* (July/August 1984): p. 48-55. See also Peter Warren, "Minoan Crete and Ecstatic Religion: Preliminary Observations on the 1979 Excavations at Knossos," in *Sanctuaries and Cults in the Aegean Bronze Age,* ed. Robin Hägg and Nanno Marinatos (Stockholm: Svenska Institutet i Athen, 1981).

22. Castleden, *Knossos Labyrinth,* pp. 121-22.

23. Riane Eisler, *The Chalice and the Blade: Our History, Our Future* (San Francisco: Harper and Row, 1987), p. 188.

24. Lynn White Jr., "The Historic Roots of our Ecologic Crisis," *Science* (March 1967): 1207ff.; Spretnak, ed., *Politics of Women's Spirituality,* pp. xii.

25. John P. Ferguson, "The Great Goddess Today in Burma and Thailand: An Exploration of Her Symbolic Relevance to Monastic and Female Roles," in *Mother Worship: Themes and Variations,* ed. J. P. Preston (Chapel Hill: University of North Carolina Press, 1982), p. 295. See also Mi Mi Khiang, *The World of Burmese Women* (Totowa, N.J.: Zed Press, 1986).

26. See Ena Campbell, "The Virgin of Guadalupe and the Female Self-Image: A Mexican Case History," in *Mother Worship,* ed. Preston.

27. Marina Warner, *Alone of All Her Sex* (New York: Knopf, 1976), p. 283; Campbell, "The Virgin of Guadalupe," p. 21; Ehrenberg, *Women in Prehistory,* pp. 22-23; Sarah Pomeroy, *Goddesses, Whores, Wives and Slaves: Women in Classical Antiquity* (New York: Schocken, 1975), p. 15.

28. Gimbutas, "Proto-Indo-European Culture," p. 155.

29. Charlene Spretnak, *The Spiritual Dimension of Green Politics,* (Santa Fe, N.M.: Bear & Co.), p. 32.

30. Ibid., pp. 32-33; *The Nation,* "Letters" section, 2 April 1988, p. 476; "Introduction," *Politics of Women's Spirituality,* p. xiv.

31. Milisauskas, *European Prehistory,* pp. l3l, l83, l85, l90.

32. Ibid., p. 185.

33. Colin Renfrew, "The Origins of Indo-European Languages," *Scientific American* (October 1989): 106-114, at 109, 110.

34. Milisauskas, *European Prehistory,* pp. 113-14.

35. Renfrew, "Origins," p. 109.

36. Colin Renfrew, *Before Civilization: The Radiocarbon Revolution and Prehistoric Europe* (Cambridge University Press, 1973, 1979), pp. 151-59.

37. Leacock, "Women in Egalitarian Societies," pp. 32-33.

38. Bookchin, *Ecology of Freedom,* p. 62.

39. See *Ecology of Freedom* for Bookchin's account of the rise of hierarchy.

40. Ynestra King, "Ecological Feminism," *Z* (August 1988): 124.

41. Barbara S. Lesko, "Women in Egypt and the Ancient Near East," in *Becoming Visible,* ed. Bridenthal, Koonz, and Stuard, pp. 43, 48, 50.

42. See Starhawk's account of the rise of hierarchy in her *Truth or Dare.*

43. James Mellaart, *Çatal Hüyük: A Neolithic Town in Anatolia* (New York: McGraw-Hill, 1962), p. 202.

44. Renfrew, *Before Civilization,* pp. 180-82.

45. Merlin Stone, *When God Was a Woman* (New York: Harcourt, Brace, Jovanovich, 1978), p. 130.

46. Prentice, "Taking Sides: What's Wrong with Eco-Feminism," pp. 9-10.

47. Ibid., p. 10.

48. King, "Healing the Wounds," in *Reweaving the World,* ed. Diamond and Orenstein, p. 109.

Nietzsche, ed. Monroe C. Beardsley (New York: Modern Library, 1960), p. 315.

33. Merchant, *Death of Nature,* p. 280.

34. Leibniz, *Discourse on Metaphysics* IV, trans. George R. Montgomery, in *European Philosophers,* ed. Beardsley, p. 253.

35. John Herman Randall, Jr., *The Making of the Modern Mind: A Survey of the Intellectual Background of the Present Age,* rev. ed. (Boston: Houghton Mifflin, 1940), p. 297.

Chapter 4
Mythopoesis and the Irrational

l. Susan Griffin, "Split Culture," first published in *The Schumacher Lectures,* vol. 2, ed. Satish Kumar, London. Blond & Briggs, 1984; reprinted in *Healing the Wounds,* ed. Plant, pp. 7-17, at 11, 19, 9.

2. Spretnak, "Toward an Ecofeminist Spirituality," p. 127.

3. Starhawk, *The Spiral Dance* (San Francisco: Harper and Row, 1979), pp. 7, 13, 25; also, "Witchcraft as Goddess Religion," in *Politics of Women's Spirituality,* ed. Spretnak, p. 49.

4. Starhawk, *Truth or Dare,* p. 104.

5. Eisler, *Chalice and the Blade,* pp. l83-84, 202.

6. Starhawk, *Spiral Dance,* p. 196.

7. Starhawk, *Truth or Dare,* p. 269.

8. Deena Metzger, "Invoking the Grove," in *Healing the Wounds,* ed. Plant, p. 124.

9. Murray Bookchin, "Ecology and Revolutionary Thought," 1965; reprinted in *Post-Scarcity Anarchism,* Montreal: Black Rose Books, 1977.

10. Frankfort, H. and H. A., "Myth and Reality," in *Before Philosophy,* ed. Frankfort and H. and H. A., p. 20.

11. Marjorie Nicholson, *The Breaking of the Circle: Studies in the Effect of the "New Science" upon Seventeenth-Century Poetry* (Evanston, IL.: Northwestern University Press, 1950), p. xix.

12. On correspondences, see ibid.; Bethell, *Cultural Revolution of the Seventeenth Century;* Spencer, *Shakespeare and the Nature of Man.*

13. Merchant, *Death of Nature,* p. 288.

14. Spretnak, "Toward an Ecofeminist Spirituality," p. 129.

15. Lee Quinby, "Ecofeminism and the Politics of Resistance," in *Reweaving the World,* ed. Diamond and Orenstein, pp. 122-23.

16. Blumenfeld, "What Is to Be Undone," p. 19.

17. Starhawk, "Power, Authority and Mystery," p. 76.

18. Nicholson, *Breaking of the Circle,* p. 106.

19. Spretnak, "Toward an Ecofeminist Spirituality," p. 132.

20. Christ, "Rethinking Theology and Nature," p. 69.

21. King as quoted in Luhrs, "Women, Peace, and Ecology," p. 10; King, "Ecology of Feminism," p. 23; and "Coming of Age with the Greens," *Z* (February 1988): 19.

22. King, "Healing the Wounds," in *Reweaving the World,* ed. Diamond and Orenstein, p. 120.

23. Sharon Doubiago, "Mama Coyote Talks to the Boys," in *Healing the Wounds,* ed. Plant, p. 41.

24. Susan Sontag, "Feminism and Fascism: An Exchange," *New York Review of Books,* 20 March 1975, pp. 31-32.

25. Griffin, "Curves Along the Road," p. 92.

26. Himmler quoted in Robert A. Pois, "Man in the Natural World: Some Implications of the National-Socialist Religion," in *Political Symbolism in Modern Europe: Essays in Honor of George L. Mosse,* ed. Seymour Drescher et al. (New Brunswick, N.J.: Transaction Books, 1982).

27. Griffin, "Split Culture," p. 10.

28. See John de Graaf, "The Wandervogel," *Co/Evolution Quarterly* (Fall 1977): 14-21.

29. Christopher Lasch, *The Minimal Self: Psychic Survival in Troubled Times* (New York: W. W. Norton, 1984), p. 34.

30. Merchant, *Death of Nature,* p. 288.

31. Blumenfeld, "What Is to Be Undone," p. 28.

32. John Mohawk, lecture delivered at Institute for Social Ecology, Plainfield, Vermont, June 26, 1989.

Chapter 5
Dialectics in the Ethics of Social Ecology

1. R.G. Collingwood, *The Idea of Nature* (Oxford: Clarendon Press, 1945, reprinted New York: Oxford University Press, 1978), p. 6; John Herman Randall, Jr., *Aristotle* (New York: Columbia University Press, 1960).

2. John Herman Randall, Jr., *The Making of the Modern Mind* (Boston: Houghton Mifflin, 1926, 1940), p. 269.

3. Bookchin, *Ecology of Freedom,* pp. 234-35.

4. Randall, *Making of the Modern Mind,* p. 269.

5. Bookchin, *Ecology of Freedom,* pp. 285-86.

6. Ibid., p. 238.

7. Ibid., p. 161.

8. Max Horkheimer, and Theodor Adorno, *Eclipse of Reason* (New York: Oxford University Press, 1947), p. 97.

9. Jonas, *Gnostic Religion,* p. 323.

10. Bookchin, *Ecology of Freedom,* pp. 270, 165.

11. Ibid., p. 271.

12. Corinne Kumar d'Souza, "A New Movement, A New Hope: East Wind, West Wind, and the Wind from the South," in *Healing the Wounds,* ed. Plant, pp. 29-39.

13. Bookchin, *Ecology of Freedom,* p. 274.

14. Ibid., pp. 235, 273.

15. Ibid., p. 235.

16. On dialectical naturalism, see Murray Bookchin, *The Philosophy of Social Ecology,* (Montreal: Black Rose Books, 1990). The following discussion is based largely on this book.

17. Ibid., p. 30.

18. Ibid, p. 28.

19. Ibid., p. 31.

20. See G.W.F. Hegel, *The Logic,* translated from *The Encyclopaedia of the Philosophical Sciences* by William Wallace, 2d ed., rev. (London: Oxford University Press, 1968), 1873.

21. On the ethics of social ecology, see Bookchin, *Ecology of Freedom* and *The Philosophy of Social Ecology.*

22. Chiah Heller, "Toward a Radical Eco-Feminism" in *Renewing the Earth: The Promise of Social Ecology,* ed. John Clark (London: Greenprint, 1990).

Chapter 6
Women in Democratic Politics

1. Judith Plant, "Searching for Common Ground: Ecofeminism and Bioregionalism," in *Reweaving the World,* ed. Diamond and Orenstein, p. 160; Catherine Keller, "Women Against Wasting the World: Notes on Eschatology and Ecology," in *Reweaving the World,* ed. Diamond and Orenstein, p. 262.

2. Cynthia Hamilton, "Women, Home, and Community: The Struggle in an Urban Environment," in *Reweaving the World,* ed. Diamond and Orenstein, p. 217.

3. Diamond and Orenstein, "Introduction," in *Reweaving the World,* ed. Diamond and Orenstein, p. x.

4. Bookchin, *Ecology of Freedom,* p. 138.

5. Diamond and Orenstein, "Introduction," p. x.

6. Unidentified feminist and environmental activist paraphrased by Mark Satin in "Plant and Diamond: An 'Ism' Is Born," *New Options* (August 27, 1990): 8; Anne Cameron, "First Mother and the Rainbow Children," in *Healing the Wounds,* ed. Plant, p. 64.

7. Hamilton, "Women, Home, and Community," p. 222.

8. King, "Healing the Wounds," in *Reweaving the World,* ed. Diamond and Orenstein, p. 116; King, "Coming of Age with the Greens," p. 18.

9. Caroline Estes, "An Interview with Caroline Estes: Consensus and Community," in *Healing the Wounds,* ed. Plant, pp. 236, 241.

10. Ibid., pp. 241, 234.

11. Helen Forsey, "Community—Meeting Our Deepest Needs," in *Healing the Wounds,* ed. Plant, p. 234.

12. Arisika Razak, "Toward a Womanist Analysis of Birth," in *Reweaving the World,* ed. Diamond and Orenstein, pp. 168, 166, 172.

13. Michelle Zimbalist Rosaldo, "Woman, Culture, and Society: A Theoretical Overview," in *Woman, Culture, and Society,* ed. Michelle Zimbalist Rosaldo and Louise Lamphere (Stanford, Ca.: Stanford University Press, 1974), p. 36.

14. Bookchin, *Ecology of Freedom,* p. 54.

15. Ibid., p. 149.

16. See Suzanne F. Wemple, "Sanctity and Power: The Dual Pursuit of Early Medieval Women," in *Becoming Visible,* ed. Bridenthal, Stuard, and Koonz, pp. 147-49.

17. Murray Bookchin, *The Politics of Cosmology,* unpublished ms., p. 91.

18. Mary D. Dietz, "Context Is All: Feminism and Theories of Citizenship," *Daedalus* (Fall 1987): 1-24, at 15.

19. On libertarian municipalism, see Murray Bookchin, *The Rise of Urbanization and the Decline of Citizenship* (San Francisco: Sierra Club Books), 1987.

20. Dietz, "Context Is All," pp. 14-15.

21. Judith Plant, "The Circle Is Gathering...," in *Healing the Wounds,* ed. Plant, p. 245.

Index

A

abortion, 127-28
Adam, 71
aesthetic sensibility, 87
"aliveness" of nature.
  See hylozoism
Amos 62
"ancients-moderns" quarrel, 72-73
Aquinas, Thomas, 17
Aristotle, 16, 17, 65, 82, 106
Athens, democratic *polis* of, 65, 135-36, 140, 145-48. 156
Augustine, 17, 65, 69
Augustus, 67

B

Bachofen, Jacob, 39
Beauvoir, Simone de:
  repudiates "new femininity," 16
  on woman as "other" in *Second Sex,* 14-15
Beethoven, Ludwig van, 7
belief, 93-96
Bergson, Henri, 74
Blumenfeld, Gina:
  on magic, 91
  on utilitarianism, 20
  on women and reason, 103
Bookchin, Murray, 5, 21
  dialectical naturalism of, 117-24
  on democratic *polis,* 146-47
  on development of hierarchy, 46-47
  and ecological ethics, 22
  on ecology's critical thrust, 86, 126
  on emergent subjectivity, 116
  on ethics of social ecology, 125-29
  on forms of freedom, 135
  on household in Neolithic society, 31
  on instrumentalism, 107, 111-12, 113, 132
  on kinship society, 143
  on science and natural order, 107, 108, 109
  on worship of goddess in organic society, 34
  See also social ecology
Boorstin, Daniel, 101
bureaucratization, 109-110
Butterfield, Herbert, 72

C

Cameron, Anne, 133
Campbell, Ena, 41
Campbell, Joseph, 43
capitalism, 51, 52, 109, 151
  ethics of competitive marketplace, 109-10
  organismic metaphors for, 102
  and women, 54
Caracalla, Emperor, 149
"caring" and "nurturing":
  ethos of, 24
  hierarchy and, 144-45, 149
  in Neolithic societies, 50
  needed by society, 12
  particularity of, 148-49
  patriarchal stereotypes and, 15-16
  and women, 2, 110, 154-55
Carson, Rachel, 4
Castleden, Rodney, 37
Çatal Hüyük:

disappearance of Neolithic culture of, 44
figurines found in debris, 35
goddess worshipped in Neolithic, 34
priestesses in, 49
Chain of Being, Great, 67-68
Chipko "tree-hugging" movement, 4
Christ, Carol P., 67, 94
Christianity, 2, 17, 48, 69, 106
Cicero, 66
Clamshell Alliance, 138
coherence, 3, 19, 90
Collard, Andrée, 2, 19
contradictions in, 18
Rape of the Wild, 2, 18
on women's reproductive biology, 11
Collingwood, R. G., 65, 66, 69, 106, 107
community:
decline of, 110, 132-36
need for preservation of, 11
See also democratic process; democratic tradition
confederation, 151-52
"correspondences," 70-73, 88, 106, 120
cosmology
Egyptian, 59
hylozoism as, *see* hylozoism
Mesopotamian, 60-61
medieval, 68-69
Crete, Minoan, 23, 30, 31, 36-39, 84
goddess worship in, 37
human sacrifice in, 38-39
Knossos as temple in, 37-38
priestess elite in, 37-38, 49
"cult of true womanhood," 110, 131

D

Daly, Mary, 2, 9
Darwin, 78
De Beauvoir, Simone. *See* Simone de Beauvoir

deep ecology, 3, 4, 22
Demeter, 89
democratic process, 136-37, 153-54
and dissent, 138
and personal affairs, 153
virtues of, 153-54
democractic tradition, 134-35
ecofeminism and, 135-36
and libertarian municipalism, 150-57
potential inclusiveness of, 149, 155-56
women and, 150-57
Democritus, 65
dependency, human,
on biosphere, 11
Descartes, René, 106, 108
dialectical naturalism, 117-24
dialectics, Hegelian, 120-21, 122-23
dialectics, Marxian, 123
Diamond, Irene, and Gloria Orenstein, 2, 9
and ethic of interconnectedness, 22
on women and community issues, 132, 133
Dickinson, Emily, 7
Diderot, Denis, 120
Dietz, Mary, 149, 152
domestic realm, 23, 110, 131-33, 139-41
and public realm:
in history, 141-46
in social ecology, 150, 155-57
Doubiago, Sharon, 95
Driesch, Hans, 74
d'Souza, Corinne Kumar, 112-13
dualism, mind-body, 17, 119-20

E

earth, as "mother," 13, 69
Homeric Hymn to, 13
ecological ethics, 21-22, 95-96, 109, 124-29
eduction, 123
Egypt, ancient:

divine immanence in cosmology of, 59
hierarchy in, 60
women in, 48
Ehrenberg, Margaret, 31-32
on matrilocality and matrilineality, 31
on relationship between goddess worship and status of women, 41
on sympathetic magic and female figurines, 35-36
Eisler, Riane, 29
on hylozoism, 57
on images and myths, 40
on Minoan Crete, 36
on power of myth, 83-84
on reclaiming Neolithic traditions, 30-31
Elizabeth I, 71
Engels, Frederick, 123
Enlightenment, 94
Epictetus, 67
Epicurus, 65
Erigena, John Scotus, 87
Estes, Caroline, 137-39
ethics:
divine immanence and, 57-64
ecological, 21-22, 124-29
erosion of old systems of, 109
falsehood and, 95-96
hylozoism and, 77-80
in kinship society, 142-43
Euripides, 17
Europe, Neolithic, 2, 29-36, 84, 100, 141
and ecological ethics, 23-24
goddess worshipped in, 33-36
hierarchy in, 49
household in, 31
human sacrifice in, 32-33
Linear Pottery Culture in, 31, 45
matrilineality and matrilocality in, 31-32, 50, 142
myth of, 29-32
peacefulness of, 32
social factors in, 41-42

Evans, Sir Arthur, 36-37
Eve, 17
evolution, 113-17, 123-24
inorganic, 114-15
organic, 115-17

F

fascism, 99-100
female figurines, 29
found in debris, 35
possible use in sympathetic magic, 35-36
Ferguson, John, 40
Filmer, Robert, 52
final cause. See teleology
Firestone, Shulamith, 10
Forsey, Helen, 139
Fox-Genovese, Elizabeth, 44-45
Frankfort, Henri, 59, 60
and H.A. Frankfort, on mythopoesis, 87
freedom:
forms of, 135
See also democratic process; democratic tradition
free nature, 126-27

G

Gaia (goddess), 13
Gaia hypothesis. See hylozoism
gender, in natural history, 128-29
Gibbs, Lois, 132
Gimbutas, Marija, 31
on human sacrifice, 32
on Indo-European Earth Mother, 33-34
and "Kurgan" invasion theory, 42, 43, 44, 45
and "Old Europe," 30
religious interpretation of data of, 33
god, Hebrew conception of, 61-63, 78
goddess, 14, 29, 97
as consumer item, 100-104
existence of, 93
and "oneness," 82-83

order in, 106
Neolithic Europe. *See* Europe,
Neolithic
Nero, Emperor, 67
"new stars," 72
Nicholson, Marjorie Hope, 88, 93

O

oikos. See domestic realm
"oneness," 82-83, 117
order in nature, 106
organic societies, 20
"other," women as, 14-16

P

patriarchal stereotypes, 15-16,
  25-27, 97-98
  immutable female nature, 25-
  27
  "otherness" and, 14-16
Plant, Judith, 2
  on "home," 131
  metaphor and, 19
  "otherness" as nondualistic
  epistemology, 15
  and "women's values," 22, 23,
  131
Plato, 16, 65, 69, 106
Plotinus, 65
polis, 135-36, 140, 146-48, 156
  exclusions of, 148
politics:
  contrasted with statecraft, 150
  new realm of, 150-57
Pomeroy, Sarah:
  on Knossos excavation, 36-37
  on relationship of goddess
  worship and status of women,
  41
Potnia, 37
priestesses:
  as elite in Minoan Crete, 38
  as hierarchical, 48-50, 61
primary oppression, theory of,
  47-56
private realm, 44. *See also* domestic realm

psycho-biologistic ecofeminism,
  11-14
public realm
  in history, 141-46
  in social ecology, 150, 155-57

Q

Quinby, Lee, 90

R

racism, 51, 53
Raleigh, Walter, 70-71
Randall, John Herman, Jr., 106,
  107
Randi, James, 91-92
randomness, 114-15
Razak, Arisika, 139-40
reason, human:
  and order in the natural world,
  106
  dialectical, 117-24, 120-23
  hypothetico-deductive, 106
  importance of, 103-104, 154
  instrumental, 111-112
  women's:
  ethics of social ecology and,
  127
  as human birthright, 103
  lacks authority, in Aristotle,
  16
Renfrew, Colin:
  critical of "Kurgan" invasion
  theory, 44, 45
  on possible religious hierarchy in Old Europe, 49
Rosaldo, Michelle Z., 142
Russell, Bertrand, 108

S

sacrifice, human:
  in Minoan Crete, 38-39
  in Neolithic Europe, 32-33
Scientific Revolution, 2, 48, 70,
  107-109
scientism, 112-13
Scot, Reginald, 138
Semonides, 17

senescence. *See* hylozoism, decay of nature as
sexual liberation, 10
social constructionism, 3, 17-19,
social ecofeminism, 5
social ecology, 3, 4, 5, 22
  antihierarchical, 6-7
  dialectics in, 105
  dialectical naturalism of, 117-24
  domestic realm in, 150-155-57
  as eco-anarchism, 6
  ethics of, 124-29
  first and second nature in, 117-18, 125-26
  free nature in, 126-27
  libertarian municipalism of, 150-57
Socrates, 106
Sontag, Susan, 98-99
Sorel, George, 85
Spencer, Theodore, 67, 68, 71
Spretnak, Charlene, 41, 45
  on "Kurgan" invasions, 43
  on Neolithic, 24
  on "oneness," 82
  psycho-biologism of, 13-14
  religious determinism of, 40
Starhawk, 22, 68, 101
  and "aliveness" of the earth, 23
  on development of hierarchy, 49
  and divine immanence, 58-59, 62
  and hylozoism, 57-58, 73, 77-78
  and interconnectedness as value, 22
  and intuition, 83
  on magic, 85-86, 91
  on progress, 30
  on "worldview of power-over," 60-61
state:
  development of, 51-52, 109
  dual power to, 151
  and women, 54

Stone, Merlin, 36, 49
subjectivity, 116-17
sympathetic magic, 35-36

T

teleology, 107-108
Tertullian, 17
Tinker Bell, 95
Tringham, Ruth, 33

U

universalism, 112-13
utilitarianism, 96-98

V

vitalism, 74-77
Voltaire, 77

W

Warner, Marina, 41
Warren, Peter, 38-39
Weyer, Johann, 138
White, Lynn, 40
Wollstonecraft, Mary, 9
"woman-nature" metaphors, 4, 85, 89, 97-98, 154
women:
  associated with nature, 12-13
  biology of, 9, 10, 154
  and democratic tradition, 155-57
  in Egypt, 48
  in Mesopotamia, 54
  as "other," 14-16
  status of, and goddess worship, 39-41
  See also "caring and nurturing"

X

Xenophanes, 93

Z

Zeus, 13, 136

About South End Press

South End Press is a nonprofit, collectively run book publisher with over 150 titles in print. Since our founding in 1977, we have tried to meet the needs of readers who are exploring, or are already committed to, the politics of radical social change.

Our goal is to publish books that encourage critical thinking and constructive action on the key political, cultural, social, economic, and ecological issues shaping life in the United States and in the world. In this way, we hope to give expression to a wide diversity of democratic social movements and to provide an alternative to the products of corporate publishing.

If you would like a free catalog of South End Press books or information about our membership program—which offers two free books and a 40% discount on all titles—please write us at South End Press, 116 Saint Botolph Street, Boston, MA 02115.

To order this, or any other South End Press title, please call 1-800-533-8478.

Other titles of interest from South End Press:

Remaking Society
Murray Bookchin

Defending the Earth:
a Dialogue Between Dave Foreman and Murray Bookchin
with an Introduction by Steve Chase and Foreword by David Levine

Race, Gender, and Work: A Multi-Cultural Economic History
of Women in the United States
Teresa Amott and Julie Matthaei

Yearning: Race, Gender, and Cultural Politics
bell hooks

Walking to the Edge: Essays in Resistance
Margaret Randall

Women, AIDS, and Activism
ACT UP/NY Women and AIDS Book Group